# Flickers

*An Illustrated Celebration*
*of 100 Years of Cinema*

Gilbert Adair

*faber and faber*
LONDON · BOSTON

# Contents

# Introduction

This book absolutely does not purport to be a history of the cinema (an aspiration which, in view of the by now unimaginable wealth of material, has far outstripped the competence of any one critic, however well informed); nor is it an inventory of the 'hundred greatest films ever made', whichever they might be; nor would its anthology of stills claim to be in any sense 'definitive'. Its ambition is the rather more modest one of celebrating, and at the same time interrogating, an unashamedly personal selection of images from a century of cinema, images which have spoken to me over the half-century of my own life, as have the films to which they belong, images which continue to speak to me even now. And since it would be vain to pretend that the book's primary *raison d'être* is not the medium's centenary – dated here, as it conventionally is, from the very first public screening of the work of Auguste and Louis Lumière in 1895 (but the cinema, in truth, like many an ageing actress, is a few years older than it cares to admit) – I suggest that the reader regard the relation of each image to the year in question as exactly that which an individual candle on a birthday cake bears to the year it represents.

The organizing principle I have laid down for myself is that each of the cinema's hundred years be represented by a single film and a single still. There are therefore, of necessity, numerous, regrettable injustices: no *L'Atalante,* no *Night of the Hunter,* no Dovzhenko, Guitry, Wilder, Sirk, Mankiewicz, Kurosawa, Kiarostami or Nicholas Ray; no Garbo, Monroe or James Dean; no African or Latin American cinema at all. (Since I obstinately believe that the presence of what film students know as an *auteur* – a director who contrives against the odds to invest his material with at least a trace of his own sensibility – is a necessary if not always sufficient prerequisite of a film's interest, the vast majority of stills selected conform to this bias.) There are ostensible omissions, too, about which, however, I am not prepared to offer an apology: thus no Riefenstahl, Rosi, Roeg, Herzog or Jane Campion; no *Gone With the Wind, Casablanca* or *Jean de Florette.* It is, I repeat, a wholly personal, unapologetically partisan choice: I am not only the author but, as it were, the *auteur* of *Flickers.*

But why, precisely, *Flickers*? Because film flickers as it traverses a projector at twenty-four frames a second. Because the eye flickers as it registers a strip of moving imagery. Because, were one to take a still from every film ever made and array them chronologically, page by page, in a book, the result would be a monstrous flicker album of the cinema's history. (This book is an unavoidable contraction of that lovely fantasy, but flicking through it will still, I think, communicate a sense of the medium's inexorable evolution.) And because, ultimately, film itself has been flickering for a hundred years now, flickering like a great fire in the grate of the cinema screen, around which millions of us have warmed ourselves, gazed dreamily into the flames and occasionally got burnt.

1

# 1895 La Sortie des usines Lumière
## *Workers Leaving the Lumière Factory*

Let there be light!

Imagine, if you will, the boulevard des Capucines, Paris, France, a December evening in 1895, the Grand Café, thirty or so Van Gogh chairs laid out in rows before a small white linen screen, a screen smaller, far, far smaller, than what we have become used to since, but that same screen, nevertheless, on which were to be imprinted the myths, dreams, drives, lies, desires, archetypes, whimsies, crotchets, psychic megrims, and occasionally the history, of our century, the first page, the frontispiece, you might say, of a volume of white screens that would be more massive, in its palmiest days, than the Bible, Gibbons, Tolstoy and Proust's *Recherche,* his *roman-fleuve,* his *roman-Mississippi,* put together, a screen on which materialized, that December evening, out of a flickering fog of capricious and irregular device (although not much more capricious and irregular, in truth, than what we still sometimes have to put up with inside a cinema auditorium), a skein of images – amazing moving images! – of workers strolling out through the main gates of a Lyonnais photographic plant.

*La Sortie des usines Lumière* or *La Sortie des ouvriers de l'usine Lumière* or even just *La Sortie des ouvriers* or, in English, *Workers Leaving the Lumière Factory* or *Lunch Break at the Lumière Factory* – the film never really had or needed a proper title. And, when viewed today, its interest tends to be a strictly specialized one, except in so far as the first of something, of *anything,* is always mysteriously beautiful – like the fabled first wheel which, if some farmer ploughing a field in south-west France, let's say, chanced to turf it up, would be more than able to hold its own in the Louvre against the Vénus de Milo and the Victoire de Samothrace.

It was the first all right – but the first of precisely what? *Les frères* Lumière, Auguste and Louis, seem not to have known themselves. (Still less did Thomas Alva Edison, whose analogous invention, a peephole machine which he christened the Kinetoscope, he somehow never got around to patenting.) Even after the triumphant screening in the boulevard des Capucines, even after the sensation of *L'Arrivée d'un train en gare de La Ciotat,* whose spectators nearly swooned away at the image of the locomotive that appeared to be hurtling directly towards them, even after *L'Arroseur arrosé,* the world's very first fiction film, a comic short about a gardener hosed down with his own hose that was remade umpteen times before the turn of the century, they persisted in attaching greater importance to their concurrent if now forgotten research into colour photographic stock.

I don't any longer recall if it was one of *les frères* Lumière or Edison or all three who made the notorious forecast that what they had come up with had not the slightest artistic potential and would never amount to more than a freaky side-show attraction. But, no matter who said it, whether it was Auguste or Louis or Thomas Alva or None of the Above, some other poor benighted chump of a genius, perhaps, of whom no one has ever heard – the point is, whoever it was, he got it *wrong*. And the point of this book is to show by just how much – since that evening in Paris in 1895, when film was brought to public light (or *lumière*) for the very first time, and notwithstanding that chronicle of false starts and dead ends that we grandly term the History of the Cinema – he got it wrong.

It's curious, the Lumières even got their subject matter wrong: the factory has never been one of the medium's favourite settings. Yet their little strip of film – running, as it does, only a few seconds – remains a profoundly affecting experience, for the genius of the cinema already flows through it like a current. *La Sortie des usines Lumière* is, after all, a work of art. It demonstrates, no less than the Lascaux cave drawings of which it may be said to be the exact filmic equivalent, the axiomatic truth that art is, ultimately, whatever lasts.

# 1896  The Kiss

Improbable as it may appear, these two performers, John Rice and May Irwin, were, of the history of the cinema, the veritable Adam and Eve, the original, only and, in sculptural configuration if not in physical condition, Rodinesque begetters of that now incalculable number of interlaced lovers, climactic clinches and happy endings by which the medium has been articulated in the ninety-nine succeeding years of its existence. Of all the kisses excised from the films screened by the projectionist played by Philippe Noiret in Guiseppe Tornatore's *Cinema Paradiso,* this was the absolute prototype.

The film in question, titled simply *The Kiss,* was produced in 1896 by Thomas Alva Edison's Manufacturing Company. (Coincidentally, the protagonist of Villiers de l'Isle-Adam's bizarre novel of scientific anticipation, *L'Eve future,* published in 1886, was a fictionalized Edison, whose most spectacular invention was, precisely, the 'Eve of the future', a robot as ravishing as a film star.) It lasted quite a bit less than a minute and was based, if that's the word I'm looking for, on a long-running Broadway play, *The Widow Jones,* of which Rice and Irwin were the stars. In fact, in what might be thought of as the primitive *reductio ad absurdum* of a practice that is still current (simply *condensing,* rather than properly *adapting,* material from one medium to another), the kiss was the only element of the stage play to be transferred intact to the film version.

Thus there were several 'firsts' implicit in *The Kiss.* It contained – or rather, was – the very first screen kiss (a kiss on the lips, note, as though kissing anywhere else would be as insipid an experience as smoking without inhaling). It was, equally, the first 'literary' adaptation in a medium that would know many, many others. Not least, it launched what we call the star-system, and the, concomitant processes of identification (we cannot resist projecting ourselves into the image that is being projected before us) and apprenticeship (we assimilate some of the more indispensable little social graces by studying how actors deal with them on the screen) on which the popular appeal of the movies continues largely to be founded.

It was also the first film (in 1896, remember!) to be regarded as risqué enough to prompt calls for censorship: *The Chap Book* wrote of its subject matter, in what must be one of the first film reviews: 'In life-size it would already be bestial, but that's nothing to what can now be seen. Blown up to gigantic proportions and repeated three times, it's completely repugnant.' Perhaps not so surprisingly, given the fairground origins of the cinema, scenes of kissing, fondling, cuddling and undressing occupied rather a lot of turn-of-the-century screen time. In the same year as *The Kiss,* for example, one Eugène Pirou obtained a success with a series of screenings of what he complacently affected to call *saynètes* (or playlets),

whose titles need no editorial comment: *Le Coucher de la mariée, Lever de Mlle Willy, Déshabillé d'un modèle;* and, in 1897, Georges Méliès (of whom we shall hear more) made a naughty *saynète* of his own, *Après le bal, le tub.* The intimate union of sex and the movies, accompanied as always by the indefatigable vigilance of the censors, the prohibitionists, the professional puritans, by the unspeakable in pursuit of the unbeatable, had been consummated.

For, as these censors started, they meant to go on. From Thomas Alva Edison's *The Kiss* to Nagisa Oshima's *In the Realm of the Senses,* from the Hays Code, which corseted the American cinema from the early thirties to the late sixties, to the various British statutory bodies set up to monitor 'video nasties' in the mid-nineties, they have ever attempted to stem the tide. Yet it's all invariably in vain: usage has always evolved exponentially faster than any concerted endeavour to regulate it. What is required now, as in the past, is a sense of historical perspective. In 1953 Otto Preminger's comedy *The Moon Is Blue* was refused a so-called Seal of Approval by the Hays Code because of its use of the word 'virgin' on the soundtrack. (Presumably the censors had no quarrel with virgins *per se*, but felt that any word which called attention to a woman's erogenous and egregious zones was capable of corrupting the public.) The movie, if unutterably tame by present standards, remains quite watchable; its censors, meanwhile, have gone the way of all flesh-lacerating bodies. When will they ever learn? Maybe when the moon is blue.

# 1897 Fatima's Dance

Everyone, I'm sure, will have experienced that unsettling moment, while watching a film in an auditorium, when the disposition of a character or set of characters on the screen begins inexorably to organize itself into the precise composition of a shot, a photogram, perhaps, with which we have already been made wearily familiar from the film's publicity stills – whereupon, as every last gesture, every last expression, knits into place, the narrative appears to be suspended for a split (and probably only half-conscious) second.

I have never seen *Fatima's Dance*. I don't know exactly of what her dance consists (although I'm willing to hazard a guess that it's Spanish or pseudo-Spanish in style). Yet I find this photogram, too, imbued with the eerie stillness of inevitability. Just by looking at it, I can almost *see* the fitful, choppy, scratchy flicker of the moving image as the lady sashays into her no doubt once celebrated routine. And even if I know nothing of Fatima or her dance (what, I wonder, is the story behind this brief fragment of a life?), even if, too, she is scarcely, by current svelte standards, what anyone would call beautiful, I find it very moving that she should have had the good fortune to dance her way into the history of the cinema, hence into history itself. And, as with so many of the medium's stars to come, stars whose light may well be reaching us long after their own demise, like that of the very stars in the firmament, I feel like applauding her shadow as if that shadow could actually hear my applause.

# 1898   The Battle of Manila Bay

J. Stuart Blackton was an innovator if ever there was. On an almost daily basis he filmed newsreels of street crimes, accidents and fires in turn-of-the-century New York. He had constructed, in Flatbush, Brooklyn, the world's first glass-enclosed film studio. He pioneered the single-frame technique (one movement to one frame) which is still used in animation and puppetry. Before Griffith, he understood the significance of editing in the articulation of a narrative (even if that narrative, as was frequently the case, lasted barely more than a few seconds) and devised the close shot – a shot halfway between medium and close-up. He was responsible for some of the cinema's earliest two- and three-reel comedies and also, and somewhat schizophrenically, for the first of its literary and theatrical filchings (frequently from Shakespeare, then as now). He later experimented with colour (in Britain, where he was born), became president of the record-player company Vitaphone and editor and publisher of *Motion Picture Magazine,* one of the world's first fan magazines, a precursor of *People.* And, with *Tearing Down the American Flag,* a movie made in 1898 at the height of the Spanish-American War, he invented cinematic propaganda.

Filmed in the same year, *The Battle of Manila Bay* was also one of his (and his partner, Albert E. Smith's). The Turneresque, even faintly Venetian, haze of this shot from the film has probably a lot to do with its age, with the sheer wear and tear of having endured beyond the call of duty. Yet Smith's subsequent description of the shoot is still calculated to take one aback:

> At this time street vendors in New York City were selling sturdy photographs of ships of the American and Spanish fleets. We bought a set of each and cut out the battleships. On a table, topside down, we placed one of artist Blackton's large canvas-coloured frames and filled it with water an inch deep. In order to stand the cut-outs in the water, we nailed them to lengths of wood about an inch square. In this way a little 'shelf' was provided behind each ship and on this shelf we placed pinches of gunpowder – three pinches for each ship – not too many, we felt, for a major sea engagement of this sort.

Now look at the image again. The cinema has often been described, not totally inaccurately, as a 'realist' art. It may be, however, that its fabled, if ill-defined, 'realism' has been neither more nor less than a capacity to convince us to believe that what we are seeing is real – an immemorial gift for the persuasive lie.

# 1899 A Visit to the Spiritualist

On page 149 of Roland Barthes' essay on the art of photography, *La Chambre claire* (or, in 'English', *Camera Lucida*), is a snapshot, by the photographer Alexander Gardner, of the youthful Lewis Payne in a prison cell, awaiting execution for having attempted to assassinate the American Secretary of State W.H. Seward in 1865. The caption to the photograph is brief and cruelly to the point: 'Il est mort et il va mourir.' *He is dead and he is going to die.* Payne is dead, obviously, because the photograph was taken well over a century ago; and he is going to die because it is precisely the very last hours of his earthly existence which Gardner has captured for posterity. 'It *will* happen,' Barthes observes of Payne's death, and yet, equally, 'it *has* happened'. By virtue of Gardner's photograph, we are confronted with a future which has already occurred.

Similarly, when we watch an old movie, practically any movie from even the twenties and thirties, what we see are performers caught between two tenses of death, the death which lies ahead and the death which has already taken place. When I, therefore, study this image from one of the countless crude burlesque farces made by Stuart Blackton and Albert E. Smith at the tip of the last century, an image which is, I confess, all I know of the movie in question, when I look in particular at the figure on the left of the shot, what I see is an actor who has long since become what he once only impersonated, a skeleton.

11

# 1900 Grandma's Reading Glass

First, some background. *Grandma's Reading Glass* is a British-made film shot at the very outset of the twentieth century by George Albert Smith, a member of the 'Brighton School' of filmmakers (he was actually born in Brighton in 1864). As a pioneer of trick effects, Smith was something of an English Méliès: among the titles of his films were *The Haunted Castle, Cinderella, Faust and Mephistopheles, Aladdin and the Wonderful Lamp,* etc. And, from practically the start of his involvement with filmmaking, he seems to have been obsessed with the development of colour (like, unexpectedly, many of the medium's early innovators), patenting, in 1908, a process named Kinemacolor for commercial exploitation.

What is it we see here? An eye. An eye in close-up (rendered that much closer by being framed within the camera's own mechanical iris). One of the first of thousands of eyes with which the cinema would, as it were, keep an eye on its spectators. The eye, for example, of the man in the moon in Méliès' *Le Voyage dans la lune.* The omniscient eyes of Lang's *Dr Mabuse.* Vertov's *Kino-Eye.* The old lady's shattered pince-nez in the Odessa Steps sequence of Eisenstein's *Potemkin.* The eye adroitly sliced in half in the opening sequence of Buñuel's *Un chien andalou.* Janet Leigh's glassy, sightless eye in the shower of her bungalow at the Bates Motel. Not to mention that pair of unforgettable eyes (in another of Hitchcock's films) gouged out by the birds of Saint Francis and transformed into two shadowy open mouths screaming silently for help.

Eyes are vulnerable – 'those tenuous instruments', blind Borges called them. And film is vulnerable. And it's the confrontation of two such vulnerabilities which makes the cinema so very moving a medium.

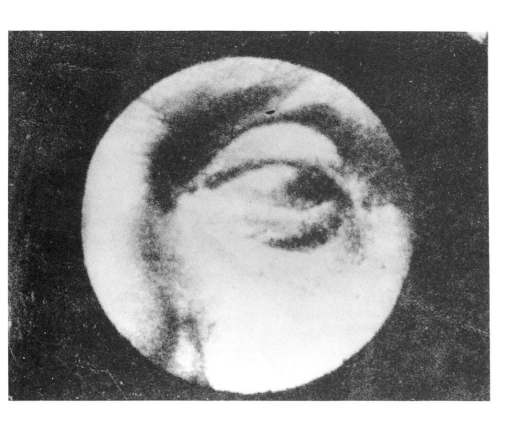

# 1901 The Execution of McKinley's Assassin

My, but things happened quickly in the cinema's early years! Just to take the example which concerns me here: President William McKinley was assassinated on September 6th, 1901, by an anarchist named Leon Szolgosz; and, a mere matter of weeks later, not only had a filmic reconstruction been produced of the assassination itself *(The Assassination of President McKinley)* but a second film had been made, covering the very last minutes, in an ominously primitive-looking electric chair, of the assassin's own life. Quite plausible the latter was too, from the evidence of the still opposite.

*The Execution of McKinley's Assassin* was also, obviously, a reconstruction, but one wonders how many spectators understood that fact or even knew what a reconstruction was. The cinema of effect and illusion has always solicited the suspension of collective disbelief; in 1901, however, that process must have operated at the most elementary level imaginable. If a film was announced as *The Execution of McKinley's Assassin* (and almost every major public event of the turn of the century was systematically 'reconstructed' by the cinema), then what audiences believed they were seeing, just as vividly as if they had been there, was neither more nor less than the real execution of McKinley's real assassin. How could it have been otherwise? How could the public of 1901 have understood that an image so real, so sinister, so unglamorous (in a medium which had already begun glamorizing its performers and sets) had actually been fabricated?

And these days? Are we so very much more sophisticated? How many people, even now, are sufficiently ciné-literate to distinguish between the slow, patient and rigorously undramatized reportages (undramatized, indeed, to the point of tedium) filmed by Frederick Wiseman and the canny and uncanny reconstructions concocted by Oliver Stone?

Stone is currently the most relevant case in point, and his *JFK,* a three-hour-long phantasmagoria on the assassination of another American President, may prove to have been something of a watershed in our media-dominated relationship with contemporary history. It had, from movie critics and political commentators alike, what is usually termed a 'mixed' press. Stone was twitted for his uncritical veneration of Kennedy, for his gullible endorsement of a ludicrously paranoid conspiracy theory (as in *Murder on the Orient Express,* 'everybody', it transpired, 'did it') and, above all, for the nonchalance with which, in a deliriously uncontrolled dialectic, he manipulated incompatible levels and layers of representation, intercutting genuine and phony newsreel

footage in such a fashion as to cow and confound all but the specialist. Not only
that but, no intellectual, he compounded the offence by defending his film as an
'alternative myth', than which it would be difficult to think of a stupider concept
or a more damning proof of his complete miscomprehension of what a myth is
and how it functions.

It would appear that, like Costa-Gavras (who made *Z, L'Aveu, Missing* and
*The Music Box*) and Francesco Rosi (best known for *Salvatore Guiliano, Lucky
Luciano* and *Illustrious Corpses*), Stone cannot envision a political narrative
unless there happens to be, at its centre, one brave, solitary individual, a star to
boot, who will single-handedly defy and vanquish the system. As with nearly all
self-styled 'political' movies, his tend to be stereotyped, academically made
thrillers which, simply because of their subject matter, one is forbidden to
dislike; as if, since the heart is in the right place, it doesn't matter where the
camera is. And what, ultimately, *JFK* recalled was that famous *Mad* magazine
cover on which a spaniel had a pistol cocked at its cute, floppy-eared little head
and the casual browser was warned: 'If you don't buy this magazine, we'll shoot
the puppy.' If you don't go and see my film, Stone seems to be threatening us,
then don't blame me if, like McKinley, like Kennedy, the President *you* voted for
is assassinated in his turn.

# 1902 Le Voyage dans la lune
## *A Trip to the Moon*

If – as I wrote in relation to the shot from *La Sortie des usines Lumière* with which this book was launched – art may be regarded, from the loftiest of overviews, as that *which lasts,* then each of the stills reproduced in it, even where the camera has functioned simply as a static, impassive recording agent, must constitute, by very definition, a fragment of filmic art. There is, however, an immediately perceptible distinction which arises with this almost too famous still from Georges Méliès' *Le Voyage dans la lune,* in that it's the first of these images reflecting indisputable evidence of what, in a rival art form, would commonly be termed a style, the external expression of a poetic cast of mind. Not only is the 'Méliès touch' already instantly identifiable, but our sense of an individual's personal appropriation and reorganization of the world (or, here, the universe), our sense that Méliès was the very first creator in the cinema's history for which such a claim may be made, is generously rewarded, is positively *pampered,* by the image in question: there's considerably more of Méliès here than of the world. And so it is, chronologically speaking, that the first significant question to be addressed on the whole problematic concept of style in the cinema – on the concept, in other words, of the director as the sole author of his films – is whether in Méliès' case this revolutionary inscription of self, of a 'personality', within the filmic image, either in motion or immobile, was gained at the expense of what has always been considered the medium's true specificity: its realism.

Viewed in this fragmented form, *Le Voyage dans la lune* appears closer to graphic art, to the cartoon strip, than to the motion picture – the photogram opposite appears, in short, to have been drawn or painted rather than filmed. It's tempting, then, to dismiss Méliès' invention of filmic style as somehow specious, something of a cheat, in so far as it could be achieved only by compelling the new art form to mimic more venerable systems of representation. Which is true enough. And yet, even if one has never seen *Le Voyage dans la lune,* even if one is incapable of mentally conjuring up, from this one still shot, the mobile face of the moon seconds before the bullet-shaped rocket lands smack in its eye or the soft splodge of contact on its cakey, icingy surface, one is surely conscious of an obscure inner tension that would not be present in any genuinely motionless image.

Méliès, a magician, caricaturist and magic-lantern showman, who had been a member of the audience at the Lumières' historic public screening of 1895 (and had in vain pleaded with the *frères* to sell their new machine to him), discovered

the art of trick photography by accident. His earliest output was in a documentary mode (he had eventually managed to buy a Bioscope projector from Robert Paul in London); and while he was shooting a straightforward street scene, his camera jammed. A few seconds elapsed before it restarted, and when he developed the film he found that passers-by miraculously disappeared and were replaced by others, motor cars leapt forward as if at the wave of a wand, the light was abruptly transformed. He had, in short, invented the articulate fireworks of special effects. *Sherlock Jr, King Kong, The Incredible Shrinking Man, Star Wars* and even *Terminator 2* are all films in the Méliès tradition.

Méliès was the first man to make a fortune in the cinema; the first, too, of many whom the cinema would bankrupt. He was the first European filmmaker to construct his own studio, at Montreuil on the outskirts of Paris, and also the first to be rewarded, as if he were a writer or a philosopher or a mathematician, with the red rosette of the Légion d'Honneur. And since *Le Voyage dans la lune* was a (free) adaptation of a novel by Jules Verne, it's perhaps fitting that, with the passage of time, Georges Méliès has come to be perceived as something of a Vernian hero himself, one of those eccentric Heath Robinson-like dreamers who contrive to change the world.

# 1903 The Life of an American Fireman

Viewed with hindsight, and whether they traded in fact or fiction, the earliest movies constituted, as it were, their own newsreel footage. Which is to say, beyond those events, genuine or staged, that they imprinted on celluloid, they were recording for posterity – in short, for us – *their own existence*, an existence that, again viewed with hindsight, was often considerably more newsworthy in itself than anything happening on the screen. When we watch the *frères* Lumière's *L'Arrivée d'un train en gare de La Ciotat*, what we really see is not so much the arriving train, or the passengers awaiting it on the station platform, but the *survival of a film*, one of the first to have been made and publicly screened. And the same is true of Edwin S. Porter's *The Life of an American Fireman*. This was an authentic turning-point in the history of the American cinema, being the very first serious and, in the terms and context of 1903, extended attempt to convey meaning through montage, to make a film less in the studio or in the streets than in the editing-room. (Which is why I have elected to illustrate it, uniquely in this book, with a composite image.) Here, too, what we really see when we watch Porter's film is the film itself, the mere but also astonishing fact that, ninety-two years after it was made, it still, heroically, exists. Everything in it that we respond to – its gravelly textures, its often mismatching photographic grain (on his editing-table Porter combined existent stock footage of fire-fighting exploits with film that, as a veritable *sniper* of imagery, he himself had shot), its fascinating sociohistorical trappings (the quaintly shaped fire-alarm kiosk, the pole leading directly from the firemen's bedroom to the attendant horse-drawn engines underneath, the spectacular rescue from a second-storey window) – we respond to in complete cognizance of the film's status as a product of technological artifice. Not for an instant, with a film so patently *old,* are we capable of suspending our disbelief; not for an instant, with a film currently viewable only in the context of a museum screening, are we capable of identifying with any of the figures we see on the screen. In this aspect, then, the cinema's most 'primitive' works paradoxically resemble its most 'modern': for we watch them today, and cannot help watching them, with a distanced, anti-illusionist, therefore truly critical eye.

# 1904 The Great Train Robbery

Edwin S. Porter's *The Great Train Robbery* was what would now be defined as an 'epic': it ran all of twelve minutes and boasted a cast of forty, the proverbial 'thousands' of its day. It was also, perhaps, the period's *Citizen Kane,* utilizing a cluster of filmic devices which were already in common currency – close-ups, cross-cutting, point-of-view shots, and so on – but with such unmatched panache that Porter seemed to have invented them (and, in fact, their absolute paternity was for many years attributed to him by film historians and critics). It had a significant influence on the supreme genius of the cinema's early history, D. W. Griffith, who would apply Porter's editing techniques to his own multi-episode epic of 1916, *Intolerance,* cutting with such breathtaking rapidity between the crucifixion of Christ and (in the movie's single modern episode) the eleventh-hour rescue of a young man about to be hanged for a crime he did not commit, that there arose, for the discombobulated spectator, a confusion as to exactly who was being rescued, the young man or Christ Himself – a confusion, to put it whimsically, between the two words 'Cavalry' and 'Calvary'. And, of course, Porter's film was a western – not the medium's first, nor its best, but as closely approaching the former as the latter to be regarded as a landmark of what was destined to become the most quintessential, and arguably the most essential, genre of the American cinema.

The image opposite is all of ninety-one years old – it is, then, far nearer the period which it depicts (the post-Civil War West) than it is to us. Yet, just as it's a still, surely, that anyone might innocently date from the nineteen-twenties or thirties or even the forties, so the movie that it illustrates already contains practically every element that would now be judged a prerequisite of the western. (And *The Great Train Robbery,* which has had so many of its once impregnable 'firsts' progressively eroded by the perpetual revision of the cinema's history, still has a claim to be the first real 'movie' – which is to say, the first popcorn-and-Coke film.) It has a raid on a telegraph office, an attack on a postal van, a chase and a climactic shoot-out.

Most amazingly, it concludes with a point-of-view shot worthy of Hitchcock (who actually re-employed it in *Spellbound*) and of Sam Peckinpah (who would employ it yet again in one of the very best and most complex westerns of recent years, *Bring Me the Head of Alfredo Garcia*) – a shot in which an outlaw draws a bead on the camera itself and fires point-blank at the spectator.

That, truly, is a first for *The Great Train Robbery.* For it was the first filmic narrative to establish what was to be the enduring link between the cinema (not only the Hollywood cinema) and the gun. Whatever the category, be it revolver, rifle, bazooka, blunderbuss, pistol, cannon or musket, and whatever the brand,

Beretta, Luger, Browning, Winchester or Smith and Wesson, the gun remains by far the cinema's single most ubiquitous prop. So ubiquitous has it become, indeed, so symbiotic appears the link between gun and camera (both hold their subjects, or victims, in their sights; both 'aim' and 'shoot'; the still camera resembles a pistol, while the movie camera might more pertinently be compared to a machine-gun), that it's difficult to name a virginally 'gunless' filmmaker. Ozu? As far as the late, gentle, extremely static comedy-dramas are concerned, almost certainly, but there are a few little-known thrillers among his silent movies. Rohmer? Not quite – muskets were visible in *Die Marquise von O . . .* Dreyer? There are no guns, to be sure, in his five great masterpieces, *La Passion de Jeanne d'Arc, Vampyr, Dies Irae, Ordet* and *Gertrud,* but he would probably have to be disqualified for having scripted the film *Ned Med Vabnene,* whose indecipherable title turns out to mean *Lay Down Your Arms.*

What *can* be stated about such an inventory is that the absence of firearms would appear to be directly linked to a notion of visual and thematic austerity and therefore that no Hollywood filmmaker has ever figured on it or is ever likely to. The blessing – as also the curse – of the American cinema, the cinema that Edwin Porter all but invented, is that it's so damned *entertaining* (a word for which, interestingly, there exists no direct equivalent in several European languages). And what Porter discovered in 1903 was that there are no better weapons for *enforcing* that entertainment than weapons themselves.

# 1905 Rescued by Rover

That title is, as the French say, *tout un programme* and has surely no need of editorial elucidation. (Even in 1905 animals were being used to add 'human' interest to a film's plotline, as aliens tend to be used now.) The film itself, though, even if simplistic in purely narrative terms, is a work of real significance, both for its technical sophistication (surprising as it may seem, it has a relatively complex structure and boasts a number of fluid panning shots and unexpected camera angles) and also as the first important product of the burgeoning British cinema, the cinema of R. W. Paul, Will Barker, Walter Haggar, Birt Acres and, the director of *Rescued by Rover* and the movement's implicit master, Cecil Hepworth.

Equally surprising is the fact that the British cinema was a prominent one in the medium's infancy. With the twentieth century but a few years old, modes of production, distribution and exhibition were established which bear an uncanny resemblance to those in force today. According to a survey published in the 1914 edition of the *Kinematograph Year Book,* Britain had over eleven hundred picture houses, more than half of them within the Greater London area. The British Board of Film Censors was set up in 1912. Film studios were constructed not only in such expected locations as Ealing, Elstree and Teddington, but in Clapham, Victoria and St. Albans as well. There existed so-called 'schools': the Brighton School, which had James Williamson as its presiding genius, was the most prestigious of its time. Hepworth's own long-running *Tilly* cycle of comedies made household names, the British cinema's first, of Alma Taylor and Chrissie White. Another series, *Winky,* featuring the comic Reggie Switz, ran up a total of thirty-nine instalments. And enterprising producers were even then ransacking the Complete Works of Shakespeare with an eye to eventual adaptation. In 1913 Sir Johnston Forbes-Robertson, the Olivier of his day, dazzled audiences with a mute and radically abridged *Hamlet,* a *Hamlet* with not much to offer *except* the Prince.

Like the recreations which they supplanted – fairground peep shows, song slides, popular novels and primitive comic-books – the very first British films were mostly unauthored artefacts, naïve, anecdotal and already derivative. One historian of our national cinema has drawn up a list of several more or less concurrent plot synopses that were all lackadaisically cribbed from the medium's earliest work of fiction, *L'Arroseur arrosé*: 'Boy treads on gardener's hose then releases the water', 'Youth grips gardener's hose then releases water', 'Boy tricks gardener by stepping on his hose then releasing water', and so forth. While priceless as documents, these cannot honestly claim to merit any close non-specialized attention. Yet, in a period when many of the innovations we now

take for granted already existed but were seldom deployed, when film, in short, as an aesthetic practice, continued to resemble one of those laws written into the statute books *but almost never enforced,* in a period, too, of course, when Proust and Joyce, Picasso and Matisse, Strauss and Stravinsky, were debating the field of artistic modernism, the mystery of the cinema is that something called *Rescued by Rover* (*Rescued by Rover*!) could so surreptitiously, yet so crucially, have laid the foundations for an entirely new form.

# 1906 La Naissance, la Vie et la Mort du Christ

## The Birth, Life and Death of Christ

It is, in truth, no sinecure being both a feminist and a *cinéphile*: Leni Riefenstahl worked for the Nazis; Marguerite Duras was primarily a writer; Dorothy Arzner and Ida Lupino were (let's face it) two bargain-basement auteurettes; Julia Solntseva, although a superb filmmaker, considered herself above all the widow of Alexander Dovzhenko and devoutly filmed the scripts he left unrealized at his death almost as if they had been bequeathed to her in his will, as if she were executing his deathbed request (just as the work of Agnès Varda tends to be bracketed with that of her husband, Jacques Demy, like a pair of matching blue and pink bathroom towels, cutely stencilled 'His' and 'Hers'); such contemporary Hollywood players as Penelope Spheeris, Kathryn Bigelow and Penny Marshall are mere hacks, as routine as any of their male counterparts; as for Yvonne Rainer, she was one of those weary troupers of the American Underground, of what the critic David Ehrenstein once dismissively referred to as 'Brakhagemarkopoulosangerjacobsgehrframptonetc', and whose failure after forty years to obtain a wider audience than that of their own circle of reciprocal admiration may be regarded as, just this once, not the fault of the rest of us. There remain, of course, Susan Seidelman and Jane Campion and Gillian Armstrong and Sally Potter and Lizzie Borden, about whose films other writers will certainly be capable of mustering up more enthusiasm than I can.

Homage, however, must be paid to Alice Guy (or Guy-Blaché), an authentic pioneer, perhaps the first filmmaker to tell a real story on celluloid – with *La Fée aux choux,* a fairy tale about children born in a cabbage patch (!), usually dated 1896 and therefore predating the earliest of Méliès' productions, whose style it rather resembles. Guy struggled to map out her own territory in what was already a male-dominated business and succeeded to a remarkable degree. By the start of the century she was turning out two one-reelers a week. In 1907, with her husband, Herbert Blaché, an Englishman, she founded a branch of Gaumont in Cleveland, Ohio. In 1910 she formed her own American production company, Solax (based in Flushing, New Jersey), and produced and directed a series of once-admired films. (I say 'once-admired' only because the majority are now lost.) And although by the twenties her career was at an end (a fact doubtless not unrelated to ingrained male prejudice), her achievement was, if very belatedly, recognized by the French government, which awarded her the Légion d'Honneur in 1953, when she was eighty years old. If ever a filmmaker

may be said to await rediscovery and reassessment, it is Alice Guy.

The image above is from *La Naissance, la Vie et la Mort du Christ*, which she co-directed with Victorin Jasset. The scene is that, of course, of the young Saint Veronica approaching the doomed Christ with her veil. I recall one popular version of the legend:

> Veronica was in her house when she heard the shouting and wailing from a crowd surrounding the soldiers who were leading Jesus to Calvary. She rose hurriedly, put her head to the door, looked over the heads of the crowd, and saw our Redeemer. Transported, beside herself, she seized her veil and threw herself into the street, quite oblivious of the insults and blows from the soldiers who pushed her back. Arriving in the presence of our Saviour, whose face poured with sweat and blood, she wiped it with her veil. All honour to you, courageous woman! The Saviour granted you the most precious gift which he could impart to any creature of this world, his portrait imprinted on your veil.

And I think of the veil of Veronica: what a magnificent metaphor for the cinema screen!

# 1907 Le Tunnel sous la Manche
## *The Channel Tunnel*

It was in 1902, in *Le Voyage dans la lune,* that Georges Méliès successfully (if, in technological detail, not quite accurately) anticipated the first manned flight from the earth to the moon, a prediction that would be realized sixty-seven years later. Which is why I thought it might be amusing to include, as a pendant to that film, an image from the same director's *Le Tunnel sous la Manche,* another example of one of his predictions eventually come true. What that title means in English is *The Channel Tunnel* (or, if you prefer, *The Chunnel*); and it could thus be said that, strictly as an exercise in futurology, it was the more impressive of the two films, since the Tunnel was finally completed all of eighty-eight years after it was made.

Seen here standing on the extreme right of the still, Méliès was to direct literally hundreds of films, and their titles alone (which is all that survive of many of them) make reference to an amazing number of devils, ghosts, fakirs, alchemists, spiritualists, automata, magicians, cabbalists, madmen, witches, Bluebeards, phrenologists, mermaids, mesmerists, ogres, prophets and wandering Jews. The existence of a Channel Tunnel was patently on that order for him, the order of pure fantasy, and his film's narrative was in fact a dream, a dream shared by Britain's King Edward VII (whose coronation in 1902 Méliès actually 'reconstructed' in his Montreuil studio, as *Le Sacre d'Edouard VII,* except that the film was made even before the event took place!) and the President of France, both of them visible in the image. A dream, I say, as was all of his work, its timeless magicality only underscored by those riveted metal sheets that were as ubiquitously present in his décors as rusting Victorian machinery and intestinally coiled piping would be, some seven decades later, in the films of his direct descendent, Terry Gilliam (whose *Adventures of Baron Munchausen* also contains a trip to the moon) – a dream replete with the cranky charm that we associate almost exclusively with the past's vision of the future, the charm, one might say, of the *conditional.*

# 1908 L'Assassinat du duc de Guise
## *The Assassination of the Duc de Guise*

Consider a single avenue of film history. In 1906 the French firm of Pathé set up the Société Cinématographique des Auteurs et Gens de Lettres with the stated brief of transferring to the screen a number of then fashionable literary and theatrical properties. (In this, the first ever recorded application of the word 'auteur' to the cinema, nothing ought to be understood, patently, beyond its literal, unpolemical meaning of 'writer'.) In 1908 two brothers, *les frères* Lafitte, founded what they called the Société Film d'Art. The Lafittes signed up Sarah Bernhardt and Mounet-Sully of the Comédie-Française and proceeded to commission screenplays from a cluster of prominent men of letters. Notable among these Films d'Art were *La Reine Elizabeth* and Dumas *fils' La Dame aux camélias,* both starring Bernhardt; Sardou's *Madame Sans-Gêne,* with Bernhardt's great rival, Réjane; and Hugo's *Le Roi s'amuse* and *Les Misérables.* Their most prestigious production, however, premièred that same year, was *L'Assassinat du duc de Guise.* It was written by Henri Lavedan, directed by André Calmettes and Charles le Bargy, and its accompanying score was composed by no less a celebrity than Camille Saint-Saëns.

Interestingly enough, most of these same novels and plays had already established their credentials as opera librettos. *La Dame aux camélias* and *Le Roi s'amuse* have survived longer as Verdi's *La Traviata* and *Rigoletto,* and Sardou lives on, only just, courtesy of the opera composers who recycled his gamy plots, Giordano with *Madame Sans-Gêne* and *Fedora,* Puccini, most famously, with *Tosca.* And it's arguably of opera rather than of the cinema that the still opposite is most reminiscent – of some turn-of-the-century production of Verdi's *Don Carlos,* let's say. It has, in short, *dated,* dated to exactly the extent that images from the theatre or the opera house always date with the passage of time (with those costumes in which only actors could feel at ease; that grimacingly 'artistic' make-up which, a mere decade or two on, fatally degenerates into hammy theatrical camp; and that self-conscious posturing characteristic of even allegedly 'great' productions or of even the very finest of actors, the Oliviers, Gielguds, Barrymores, Barraults, Gründgens and so on). It has dated in a way that images from the cinema, from the *real* cinema, seem never to date.

For, whatever its reputation at the time, *L'Assassinat du duc de Guise* was not anything approaching the real cinema. It was, instead, the prototype of a brand of 'cultural' filmmaking which is still with us and of which the two primary cardinal points have always been the Past (history is 'cultural' by definition,

whereas contemporaneity is constantly obliged to earn and re-earn its cultural status) and High Art. It's a type of cinema which leans on the Past as one of its crutches, High Art as its other crutch, and, not surprisingly, manages only to hobble. It's a type of cinema which excludes us from what might be termed the materiality of film as effectively as a sweet-shop window excludes a craning child from the goodies within – our noses are flattened against the screen. It's a type of cinema, in short, made by people and for people who at heart don't really believe in the cinema.

If *L'Assassinat du duc de Guise* remains at all watchable today, it's because, as the sort of solemn historical pageant that people who dislike the cinema as it is hold up as an example of what it *should* be, it constitutes a document of the contempt with which the intelligentsia of the period, even in France, dismissed the new art form; just as more recent endeavours to plug the cinema into so-called 'High Art' will also one day be watchable, if at all, only as documents. Paradoxically, just as nothing seems to us now as cruelly dated as a photograph from a stage production of the twenties or thirties, so nothing is set to date more rapidly in its turn than either the 'historical' or (supposedly) 'historic' movie, the sort of titanic work which ends up by sinking on its maiden voyage. And in view of the throbbing life still to be found in many a cheap and cheerful B-movie of the interwar years, it may be permissible to define the real cinema thus: as *the only art which does not date.*

# 1909  Gertie the Dinosaur

As we have already seen, nearly every genre to which the cinema would eventually accord its *titres de noblesse* was already in existence by the medium's first fifteen years or so: the documentary *à la* Frederick Wiseman (*La Sortie des usines Lumière*), the slapstick comedy *à la* Jerry Lewis (*L'Arroseur arrosé*), the sexual psychodrama *à la* Paul Verhoeven (*The Kiss*), the choreographed musical extravaganza *à la* Charles Walters (*Fatima's Dance*), the politico-historical reconstruction *à la* Oliver Stone (*The Execution of McKinley's Assassin*), the science-fiction odyssey *à la* Stanley Kubrick (*Le Voyage dans la lune*), the disaster movie *à la* Irwin Allen (*The Life of an American Fireman*), the western *à la* Budd Boetticher (*The Great Train Robbery*), the 'human interest' story *à la* Steven Spielberg (*Rescued By Rover*) and the costume picture *à la* Merchant Ivory (*L'Assassinat du duc de Guise*). And if Pat Sullivan's Felix the Cat, the Charlie Chaplin of the toons, may lay claim to being the cinema's first cartoon star, it was 1909, five years prior to Felix's début, that saw the arrival on the scene of its very first memorable cartoon character, Winsor McCay's *Gertie the Dinosaur*. (In actual fact, with magic lanterns and *ombres chinoises* dating as far back as the eighteenth century, with Joseph Plateau's invention of the excruciatingly named Phenakitoscope in 1832, with William Horner's Zoetrope of 1834 and the delightful *Pantomimes lumineuses* which Emile Reynaud screened on his Praxinoscope in 1891, kinetic animation long preceded the advent of what, in such a context, we are obliged to call live-action cinema.)

McCay was unquestionably one of the greatest American artists of the twentieth century. His most personal contribution, however, was to a medium – the comic strip – in which orthodox opinion has refused ever to detect greatness. He was the creator of *Little Nemo in Slumberland,* the most boundlessly inventive strip produced by anyone anywhere, and he was only secondarily a *cinéaste.* Yet, even in a medium as new and bewildering as the cinema was at the turn of the century, his was a considerable achievement. Gertie apart, he was responsible for an animated version of *Little Nemo* filmed in 1911; for the first full-length (if hardly what we would think of as feature-length) cartoon, *The Sinking of the Lusitania,* a harrowing piece of reportage even now (ah, how can I ever forget the shot of the young mother holding her baby at arm's length above the waves as she herself slips under for the third time!); and, finally, for one of the earliest conflations of animation and live-action sequences, thc wonderful, and wonderfully titled, *Dream of a Rarebit Fiend*. As for his graphic style, it had little in common with the practically limitless liberties taken by animators in the Disney and Tex Avery tradition (as Goya might have put it, the sleep of reason engenders cartoons) and was very much closer to the celebrated *ligne claire* of

the Belgian school of strip cartoonists, of Hergé in particular. Tintin himself might well have been a passenger on the tram that Gertie is attempting to swallow.

But why devote any serious consideration to cartoons at all? If for no other reason than that, far from being a quaintly peripheral offshoot of film history, they form an integral part of it. In a sense, cartoons are to the live-action cinema what that cinema already is, let's say, to the theatre, a further distillation and intensification of pure kinetic movement, of the displacement of figures in space, of that inexhaustible manipulation of line and form to which we give the name *mise-en-scène* and which distinguishes the medium from all others. Gertie, who belongs to the cinema's prehistory just as her biotype belongs to that of the world (was McCay aware of such an analogy?), was one dinosaur that didn't die out. Her succession, even so, should not be sought among the marauding tyrannosauri of Spielberg's *Jurassic Park*. Rather, remaining completely discrete from the mainstream, her evolution, in the Darwinian sense, would culminate in all the animated mice and ducks and cats and rabbits that have accompanied the history, and in their own weird fashion enriched the ecology, of the cinema – enriched it by reminding us that, like the planet on which it itself has been evolving, it wasn't necessarily designed for human beings alone.

# 1910  A Tin-Type Romance

I know little more of this film than its delightful title (paradigmatic of so much of the American cinema to come); its genre (the one-reel 'courtship' comedy); the names of its stars, Lou Delaney and Florence Turner (the 'Vitagraph girl'); the fact that it was directed, for the Vitagraph studio, by Laurence ('Larry') Trimble (a writer of pulp fiction who gravitated almost by chance to the movie industry while reconnoitring New York in 1910 for material for one of his stories and whose dog, Jean, hired not long after he himself was, would become the star of several Vitagraph productions); and this shot from it, of, precisely, Miss Turner in reflective mood.

And I wonder:

Would the nostalgico-mythic charm which is, for us, invested in the word 'Americana', which is, indeed, invested in the very word 'tin-type', have endured if the cinema – that of Griffith, of Ford, of Henry King and, more modestly, of Larry Trimble himself – had not so definitively captured it on celluloid *the first time around*, in movies like *The Musketeers of Pig Alley* (Griffith) and *Lightnin'* (Ford) and *Tol'able David* (King) and *A Tin-Type Romance*, when the concept was still pure, pristine and archetypal (even if the society it claimed to describe had already been eroded by poverty, injustice and corruption)?

Just how much, too, of the silent American cinema's pressed-flower charm is founded on its actresses' names? For isn't there, about the very name 'Florence Turner', something which, to anyone sensitive to such nuances, irresistibly connotes the American silent film actress (or possibly the English music-hall star, something that Turner did eventually become)? And could the same not be said of Mabel Normand, Blanche Sweet, Vilma Banky, Laura La Plante and, most evocatively, of the three Maes: McAvoy, Marsh and Murray? (Conversely, it's inconceivable that a silent actress might have been called Barbra Streisand or Michelle Pfeiffer.)

And isn't it extraordinary, the number of luminaries from the early American cinema who all but drifted into it, as Larry Trimble did, and the prehistory of whose lives was paved with the kind of eccentric, dead-end occupations with which biographies of the more ruggedly individualistic American novelists have familiarized us? Frank Capra, for example, was a newspaper peddler, banjo player, door-to-door salesman and professional gambler before becoming a film director. Hal Roach, the producer of scores of classic comic shorts, the man who performed the inestimable service of introducing Laurel to Hardy, was a failed gold prospector, on the brink of destitution, when he answered an advertisement for extras at Universal. In those days the cinema was truly an adventure.

Finally, this image, from a wholly forgotten and doubtless forgettable film – isn't it exquisite, isn't it worthy of, let's say, Caspar David Friedrich? And isn't that fact alone, somehow, rather amazing?

# 1911 Max lance la mode
## *Max Sets the Fashion*

Poor Max Linder! Having been once the most celebrated of the cinema's clowns, with his neat, contained, thin-lipped smile, his glossy black eyebrows and his dapper circumflex of a moustache, he was exposed to mustard gas early in the First World War; suffered a grave mental and physical breakdown; signed up with the Chicago-based company Essanay (Chaplin's future studio); made a cluster of American comedies (including, in 1922, a parody of Douglas Fairbanks' *The Three Musketeers* retitled *The Three Must-Get-Theres:* he played 'Dart-In-Again', needless to say, and incidentally confirmed, if confirmation were necessary, that Fairbanks himself was, after Chaplin, Keaton and Lloyd, the fourth, the d'Artagnan, if you like, of Hollywood's great triumvirate of silent clowns, his huge flashing smile as droll a prop as Keaton's lack of one); found his career, there too, dogged by consistent ill-health; made a suicide pact with his wife in 1925 and was discovered dead at her side in a Paris hotel room; then, as an artist, was utterly forgotten for almost forty years. Even in the sixties, when those films of his which had survived were restored, he tended, alas for him, to be recalled by historians primarily as a precursor, as an influence, notably on Chaplin and René Clair (who did, it's true, borrow several of his best gags), as if his own work represented a kind of experimental clearing-house whose products were not designed to be absorbed in and of themselves but existed solely to be picked apart by artists more talented than he and channelled into the all-engulfing Hollywood mainstream. Poor Max, poor Pagliacci!

If there is an element of truth in that brutal chronicle of what was, by any standard, a substantial career as performer and director (from 1911 to 1924), if Linder's films, seen today (there exist two compilations, *En compagnie de Max Linder* and *L'Homme au chapeau de soie*), strike us as slightly staid and contrived, just a tiny bit too damningly *European* by comparison with those of his American rivals, and crucially wanting in the sheer, pop-eyed dementia that is still calculated to delight us in the burlesque shorts of Mack Sennett and Hal Roach, homage nevertheless must be paid to his dandiacal grace, to his (as our image confirms) raffishly lop-sided elegance. Of Max Linder this at least can be said: that he more than anyone else was responsible for introducing to the cinema the imperishable charm of male evening dress, that silken straitjacket of top hat, white tie and tails without which it's next to impossible to imagine the future course of the medium. In that, as in so much else, poor Max set the fashion.

# 1912 Quo Vadis?

To evoke what might be called the house style of the Italian cinema in the teens of the century, a simple, barely annotated inventory of a few characteristic titles would probably be sufficient. The most famous of them all (albeit now seldom seen) was Giovanni Pastrone's epic production of *Cabiria,* filmed in 1914 and scripted by the poet, dramatist, novelist, philosopher and man of action, Gabriele d'Annunzio. (Obviously, this *Cabiria* bore no relation whatever to the near-homonymous *Le Notti di Cabiria,* a film made in 1957 by Fellini and starring his wife, Giulietta Masina, as an artless Roman prostitute.) And doubtless the most emblematic was *Gli Ultimi Giorni di Pompei* (or, in translation, Bulwer-Lytton's *The Last Days of Pompeii,* which, given how frequently it would be filmed there, became almost an honorary Italian novel). But there were also sumptuous adaptations of *Othello* and *Romeo and Juliet, Hamlet* and *Macbeth, El Cid* and *Parsifal,* as well as the historical biopics *Beatrice Cenci* and *Joan of Arc, Garibaldi* and *Anna Garibaldi.* As for Enrico Guazzoni's *Quo Vadis?* (the first cinematic version of Sienkiewicz's Nobel prize-winning novel), it was, even for that era of gigantism, a stupendous production, with its monumental décors, its literally thousands of extras and, as the film's publicity promised and the film duly delivered, its 'real lions'.

Paradoxically for a country whose most memorable legacy to the history of film was the movement known as neo-realism, the Italian cinema has been afflicted with this (crypto-Fascist?) predilection for the grandiose throughout its existence, taking it to its conclusion, a conclusion as absurd as it was logical, with the now forgotten wave of sixties *peplums,* those low-budget epic romances whose brawny Macistes and Herculeses would ripple obscene biceps beneath dainty togas. And, in fact, the cinema in general, and the American cinema in particular – from Griffith and Cecil B. DeMille via the phenomenally profitable cycle of disaster movies in the seventies to the current taste of James Cameron (and school of . . . ) for propelling minor characters through the nearest available plate-glass window – has ever been willing to indulge its public in what the French critic André Bazin termed 'the Nero complex', the spectator's secret craving to see a movie's sets, and the bigger the better, crumble to dust before his eyes. (Nero is, of course, one of the principal characters in *Quo Vadis?*) If Orson Welles was right, and the cinema is the most fabulous electric train set imaginable, then it would appear that its practitioners, like many an infant presented with a new train set, have had only one priority: to derail the train.

37

# 1913 Le Roi de l'air
## *The King of the Air*

There has always been in the cinema a mere hair's-breadth line to be drawn between the comic and the surreal: between Harpo Marx, let's say, his head lost in the curly, red clouds of his own hair, and the lascivious, eyeball-rolling, toe-sucking protagonist (played by the sublime Gaston Modot) of Buñuel's *L'Age d'or;* or else between one of Groucho's characteristically lyrical effusions to Margaret Dumont – 'When the moon comes creeping around the clouds, I'll come creeping around you. Ah, the moon and you! You wear a necktie so I'll know you!' – and the celebrated prologue (in which a woman's eye is slit along the middle with a razor just as the moon, precisely, reappears from behind a cloud) of the same director's *Un chien andalou,* a film, moreover, whose title bears little more resemblance to its content than those of *Horse Feathers* and *Duck Soup* to theirs.

This image from *Le Roi de l'air*, by Ferdinand Zecca, an epigone and sometime plagiarist of Méliès, a direct ancestor of the Czech Karel Zeman and the Anglo-American Terry Gilliam, is both comic and surreal, comic for reasons that ought to be obvious, almost too obvious, surreal because of the juxtaposition of the cartoonish contraption pedalled by the director himself and the parodically humdrum suburbia, than which nothing could be less like a cartoon, above which it so serenely floats. In that juxtaposition resides the cinema's inherent surreality, now so familiar to us as to be all but invisible – in the contiguity of the fantastic with the humdrum, the unlooked-for but strangely gratifying adjacency of that which has been consciously conjured up for the screen to that which doggedly resists being eliminated from it. Special effects (of which Zecca's flying machine is of course a primitive example) are nothing if they aren't initially grounded, as an electrical cord is grounded, in an environment of ordinariness in relation to which they may be seen as special. So it is that, in the entire oeuvre of Steven Spielberg, there doesn't exist a more magical, more surreal and more comic moment than that in *E. T.* (to which our still bears an uncanny compositional likeness) when Elliot's perfectly ordinary bike, speeding along a perfectly ordinary highway in a Los Angeles suburb, suddenly does something that is not perfectly ordinary. It takes off, and the movie takes off with it.

39

# 1914 The Perils of Pauline

It so happens that, switching on television to catch the early evening news, I regularly see the last five minutes (but never more than the last five minutes) of *Neighbours,* an Australian-based soap opera. What a revelation! For although it comes as no surprise to me that, in order to persuade me to tune in again the following evening at the same time, the show should systematically display that sense of aggressive self-preservation common to all open-ended fictions – most famously, by concluding each episode with a 'cliff-hanging' crisis – I would also have expected these crises to pay lip service, at least, to a certain social verisimilitude, expected them to respect, more or less faithfully, the modest co-ordinates of lived and observed reality in middle-class suburban life. In other words, I would have expected a typical episode to conclude with an ominous telegram arriving out of the blue, a fumblingly inarticulate declaration of love or an underage, tearfully confessed pregnancy. Not a bit of it! The endings of *Neighbours,* which are all I ever see of the show, could have been processed from a template of the most lurid, extravagant silent-movie serials: those quotation marks with which I sought to temper the literality of the word 'cliff-hanging' above are, in this context, wholly redundant. A diabetic mistakenly swallows a bottle of poison! A driver loses consciousness at the wheel of his careening automobile! A young woman wakes up with a start to find an intruder padding around her bedroom! I half expect to switch on one evening and discover another young woman being tied across a railway track by some evilly cackling swine, with the Sydney–Melbourne Express looming on the horizon.

The cinematic paradigm of this art of endings – this penchant for losing every battle (the end of each episode) but ultimately winning the war (the end of the final episode), this conception of the cinema as the medium which, when all seems lost, will have second thoughts, as it were, and find, *in extremis* and more frequently *beyond extremis,* just that belated narrative rejoinder calculated to rescue its heroine from the jaws of death or a fate worse than death – was, as everyone knows, *The Perils of Pauline,* a title which entered the language in 1914 and has remained there ever since. The director of *The Perils of Pauline* was Louis Gasnier. (Who was Louis Gasnier? He was the director of *The Perils of Pauline.* There being practically nothing else to report on his career, unless it be that he also directed the similarly alliterative *Exploits of Elaine,* comment on it tends to be frustratingly circular.) And its star was Pearl White, a former circus equestrienne (until she suffered a serious spinal injury), who, when Pauline's stock was falling, went on, naturally, to play Elaine.

More than a seldom seen film, then, or series of films, *The Perils of Pauline* constitutes a title, a mythic title, one which has come to serve as the logo, the

The "Perils of Pauline"-Ninth Episode

instantly identifiable trademark, of the genre it epitomizes. For, as witness my remarks on *Neighbours,* the serial is still with us. In the cinema, aside from a cluster of examples created by great directors, principally Louis Feuillade (*Fantômas, Les Vampires, Judex, La Nouvelle Mission de Judex* – even the titles were serialized) and Fritz Lang (*Die Spinnen, Spione,* his three *Mabuse* films and the pair of Indian romances he made in the fifties, *Der Tiger von Eschnapur* and *Das indische Grabmal,* none of which was literally a serial but all of which exploited the picaresque structure and louche poetry proper to the form), there has been a constant stream of them, from *Flash Gordon* to *Buck Rogers,* from *The Phantom* to *The Green Hornet,* from the *Star Wars* cycle to the *Indiana Jones* cycle. One might even go so far as to propose the serial, with its basic structural principles of exposition, suspension, (apparent) resolution and eleventh-hour (or, more precisely, thirteenth-hour) resurrection, as the paradigm of all populist filmmaking. And to propose, too, the image opposite, of the dazed and dazzling irruption of Pearl White on to one of the classic settings of sadistic fantasizing at the turn of the century, the sinisterly isolated railway track, as the emblematic image of our poor old, wonderful old cinema, a medium which has never entirely contrived to lose its working-class accent, a medium which drew its inspiration as much from the Grand Guignol and the penny dreadful as from the allegedly higher-minded virtues of Sardou and Galsworthy, a medium which was born on the wrong side of, precisely, those tracks.

# 1915 The Tramp

To every great clown of the cinema, silent or sound, is attributable what might be called a recurrent fetish image, an image, that is, in which the quintessence of his poetics, his personal mythology, is to be located: Lloyd dangling haplessly from a vast clock face, Laurel scratching his scalp with a grin of beatific idiocy, Keaton sheltering under a bedraggled, broken-backed brolly, Groucho lurching into the frame of the screen with a leer, an obscenely curvatured spine and a phallic cigar, right up to Woody Allen expostulating with his leading lady on a crowded Manhattan street. The forerunner of all such fetish images was, of course, Charlie Chaplin's climactic stroll into the sunset (giving his right leg a shake from time to time like an infant who has wet his pants), of which the example illustrated opposite, from *The Tramp*, is only one of many in his oeuvre. If this book had had to encapsulate a century of film history by virtue not of a hundred images but of a single one, this, unquestionably, would have been it.

The unique beauty of Chaplin's art resides in the tension that it sustains between the conventionalized figure of the clown (whose codified costume of baggy trousers, flapping shoes and bulbous red nose always represented, in any case, a stylized sublimation of a tramp's tatterdemalion dignity) and a realism founded on personal experience and observation: watching Chaplin's tramp, one is made simultaneously aware of the interrelated traditions of the circus and the ghetto, of tinsel and sawdust, which is why Fellini is his direct descendant. Keaton, by contrast, is a white clown, an Auguste. Like those of Jacques Tati, his gags are brilliantly contrived but often simply too lovely, too clever, to be laughed at. They lack that fundamental component of humour, one all but ubiquitous in Chaplin's work, *vulgarity*. If Chaplin's art is vulgar, though, his is the vulgarity not of the lowest common denominator but of the *deepest* common denominator. The pathos (inevitable word) of his films is rooted in the sweatshops of the East End of London and the Lower East Side of New York. And his earliest audiences, those audiences for whom he was not a petrified icon of cinema history, as he has since become, but an adorably disreputable Everyman of the slums, were moved by him even as they laughed at him because they could identify his condition so intimately with their own.

In this real, literal sense Chaplin was incomparable. No one else – not Keaton, whose responses to his environment were those of a character out of Kafka (Buster K?); not Harry Langdon, who brought to his impersonation of a long-trousered baby something of the eerie craft of the show business transvestite; not Laurel and Hardy, sublime as they were – none of these could claim quite the universality that would be his. The basic difference between Chaplin and

42

Keaton, for example, is encapsulated in the celebrated scene of *Steamboat Bill, Jr* in which the poker-faced Keaton tries on a series of different hats, including the boater that was destined to become his trademark: he admires it on himself for an instant or two before, to our amusement and amazement, rejecting it out of hand. It's an extraordinary moment, but one in which Keaton stands outside his own public persona in order to pass ironic comment upon it: one can almost see him winking at his public. The gesture, however, is ultimately divisive. It splits the audience into two, into those who know and those who don't, something that Chaplin would never have done (not, at least, until a late professional embitterment was made manifest in films like *Limelight* and *A King in New York*).

It's arguably the case that, if Chaplin is to be judged by the standards of pure *mise-en-scène,* by the strict consideration of the visual and plastic qualities of the films for which he was responsible, as actor, director, writer and even composer, then Keaton is the more stylish, more polished and more felicitous artist. Certainly, Keaton was a very fine filmmaker, many of whose films were masterpieces, and he had, throughout a long and turbulent career, his cortège of devoted champions. But Chaplin was *greater than the cinema.* Every one of his films was a masterpiece. And his public was the world.

# 1916  Intolerance

There is a shot in Chris Marker's short science-fiction film *La Jetée* of a woman's eyelash fluttering almost but not quite imperceptibly. Nothing too remarkable about that, you might suppose, except that it happens to be the only moving image in a work that is otherwise composed exclusively of still frames. It is, in context, an unnerving instant, disquietingly unforseeable, reminding the spectator of one of those great, simple truths which need to be aired from time to time: that, prior to the invention of the cinema (more precisely, of the kinetoscopes, praxinoscopes and mechanical peepshows that formed its nostalgic prehistory), a picture was, by very definition, *something that did not move*. It was a uniformly scaled-down two-dimensional replication of the world, or of any one of innumerable alternative worlds created by artists, whose power to fascinate us derived as much from its inherent, unalterable immobility as from the charm and conviction of its scale-model colours and forms. (We refer to 'moving pictures' – an archaic expression, akin to 'horseless carriages', but still used at Oscar ceremonies and kindred formal occasions – without any longer noticing what would once have been oxymoronic and self-contradictory about such a combination of words.) In a sense, then, this book constitutes a repudiation as well as a celebration of the cinema, an unavoidable repudiation of its defining signifier: motion. And, ideally, that contradiction would be redeemed if, like Marker in *La Jetée*, I could arrange for just one of my hundred arrested, statufied images from film history unexpectedly to move, to *flicker*.

If such an effect *were* possible, the still I would select would be the one above, from D. W. Griffith's *Intolerance,* a film allegedly made by the director as an act of atonement for *The Birth of a Nation,* that apology for racism of the most abject and least defensible brand, that most detestable work of genius. *Intolerance* is, after all, a moving picture, or a series of moving pictures, and the picture with which I have chosen to illustrate it is surely the most famous of all. For the Babylonian sequences of this vast portmanteau film – still, taking inflation into account, the most expensive ever made – Griffith had a stupendous set constructed, a set that has dwarfed all others before and since (for both the silent and sound versions of *Ben-Hur,* for both the silent and sound versions of *Quo Vadis?,* for *Metropolis* and *Blade Runner, Playtime* and *Les Amants du Pont-Neuf*), and he peopled it with the already statutory cast of thousands. Even now, a full eight decades after it was built, that set, with its thousands and thousands of tiny Babylonians scurrying about it, clambering over it, this way and that, is calculated to make an unforgettable impact on the most jaundiced of spectators.

But what made, and continues to make, the greatest impact of all is the fact

that it's not only the cast that moves, *Griffith's camera moves*. Not content with having built the film set of all time, not content with showing it off to his already dazzled spectators, Griffith has his camera suddenly crane upward in a slightly tilted shot that has us catching our collective breath. And although it was far from being the first occasion on which a film camera moved (rather than confining itself to motionlessly recording motion within the frame), it was, and has remained, the most exhilarating camera movement (or camera *gesture*) of all, the more so as it strikes us as somehow unplotted, unpremeditated, as if, confronted with that fabulous set, the cameraman (the celebrated Billy Bitzer, responsible for most of Griffith's masterpieces) simply could not contain himself – as if *not even the camera itself* could resist craning to secure a better view.

# 1917 The Cure

There exist, among the cinema's innumerable literary adaptations, a few ostensibly heaven-made marriages that should nevertheless have been resisted, precisely because the source material was just too strikingly remindful of the personal mythology that the director in question had already forged for himself on the screen. In terms of its subject, its stylistic luxuriance and not least its gorgeous period accoutrements, Thomas Mann's *Death in Venice,* for example, might be regarded as a distillation of Visconti's sensibility *avant la lettre.* What point could there be, therefore, in Visconti's actually filming it, as he eventually did? If Fellini, say, or even (humour me) Jerry Lewis were to have adapted Mann's novella, the result would have been bizarre, to be sure, and almost certainly unsatisfying; but at least not everything, the basic material, the script and the *mise-en-scène,* would have unresistingly converged, as in Visconti's film, in the same direction: a genuine dialectic might have been generated between the filmer and the filmed. Likewise, Georges Franju's 1965 version of Cocteau's First World War novel *Thomas l'imposteur,* brilliant as it is, cannot quite dissipate the faint but unmistakable suspicion of redundancy, so indelibly Coctelian were Franju's own earlier films. And it was surely a miscalculation of Billy Wilder to have filmed, as tardily as in 1974, Hecht and MacArthur's farce *The Front Page.* (It had already been done by Lewis Milestone in 1931 and, as *His Girl Friday,* by Howard Hawks in 1940.) The imaginative universe of Wilder and that of *The Front Page* were too cosily similar in the first place, the play too precociously Wilderian in style, to enable the director to bring anything fresh to the material, and his version felt like nothing so much as a weary stage performance at the fag end of a long tour.

There exist, by contrast, a number of potential unions between filmmakers and writers which never were consummated, and one continues to regret that they weren't. I think of Truffaut and Jean Anouilh's play *L'Alouette (The Lark),* a dramatization of the life of Joan of Arc which, uniquely, has a happy ending, with the spirit of Joan singing in the fields of Orléans. Or Chaplin and the incomplete novel by Kafka that has generally gone under the title of *Amerika.* (It was a project long nurtured by Fellini and was filmed at last as *Klassenverhaltnisse,* or *Class Relations,* by Jean-Marie Straub and Danièle Huillet in 1984.)

It may seem odd for me to be writing again of Chaplin so soon after *The Tramp,* but what interests me is the way in which he tends to be regarded as only incidentally an *auteur,* his exclusive preoccupation behind the camera being to frame himself in front of it, shambling along some leafy suburban boulevard in the Los Angeles of the teens of the century and skidding around its corners like a

wonkily insecure roller skater. Often criticized, too, is the archaism of his cinematic technique, an archaism already evident in the early shorts that he made for Essanay and Mutual, in the sentimental waifery of his heroines (e.g. Paulette Goddard in *Modern Times,* whose elfin, barefoot raggedness would not have struck one as incongruous in a *Cinderella* pantomime) and in his outright rejection of sound for *City Lights* in 1931.

A strain of authentic modernity, however, can also be detected in his work, a modernity that would certainly have found its apotheosis in a film version of *Amerika,* as witness this astonishing still from *The Cure,* which might almost have served as an illustration to Kafka's (by 1917, still unwritten) novel. Chaplin, modern? Why not? What does it remind one of, this eerie tableau (by no means the only one in his oeuvre)? What does it remind one of, this collection of grotesques, horizontal and vertical, in full-face and profile, bearded, whiskered and clean-shaven, respectable and shady, seated, standing, lying flat out or foetally crouching under a bench? Of the dadaist box-compositions of a Marcel Duchamp, a Kurt Schwitters or a Joseph Cornell, of the curiously affecting assemblages of a Joseph Beuys, of the insidious 'making strange' of our quotidian props and accessories which has been one of the permanent aspirations of modern art.

Charlie, our contemporary – to paraphrase the critic Jan Kott on that other great modern artist, Shakespeare.

# 1918 Tih Minh

It's possible to argue that no member of the Surrealist movement – by which I mean the historical upper-case school which flourished in the interwar years – was ever a truly effective conductor of the surreal. For to subscribe publicly to the Surrealist ideal, as did, for example, Dali and Magritte and Chirico and Max Ernst and the poet and theorist André Breton among many others, was *consciously* to program the aesthetics of one's work in a field in which the *unconscious* was designed to reign supreme. The painting of a 'surrealist' picture was a conscious, therefore profoundly unsurreal, undertaking, ultimately founded, as would have been the painting of an illusionistic landscape, on that accretion of professional crafts that we term a *métier*. That the Surrealists themselves understood the logical paradox behind their movement is evidenced by the fad for 'automatic writing' – the foredoomed endeavour by the paid-up poets of Surrealism (Breton, Eluard, Soupault, etc.) to subvert, even to suspend, the conscious, incorrigibly rational processes of literary creation. Therein, however, resides another paradox. The individual least likely to achieve so total a subversion would be, precisely, the experienced, professional writer, for whom the long acquired and eventually all but 'natural' gift of prose creation would fatally risk gaining the upper hand. Thus, as I say, it may be that the only true Surrealists were those who were surrealist by chance, by ignorance or by incompetence: in painting, not Magritte and certainly not Dali but the earnest, none too gifted classicist Puvis de Chavannes, perhaps, and of course the Douanier Rousseau, a near-simpleton who once publicly declared that Picasso and he were the two greatest living painters, Picasso in 'the Egyptian style' and himself in 'the modern style'; in the cinema, not Buñuel, invariably the first name to spring to mind, but the medium's exact counterpart to the Douanier Rousseau, Louis Feuillade, a jovial, good-humoured sort of fellow who was responsible for some of the most perverse and mysterious films ever made.

Although he shot around eight hundred films, of virtually every genre, Feuillade specialized in, and is now remembered exclusively for, the multi-episode, seven-hour-long serial, the most celebrated of which was undoubtedly *Les Vampires* (which starred the sublime Musidora as the anagrammatically named Irma Vep) and the greatest, which is to say, the weirdest, most uncanny, most dreamlike, was *Tih Minh,* from which comes the image on the opposite page.

What, we wonder, as we gawp at it, what on earth led to this delirious tableau? That it makes for an arresting picture, granted – but we mustn't forget, meanwhile, that it also forms part of a narrative, of a story. So where, we ask ourselves, could it possibly have started from in order to arrive *there*? And what

in heaven's name is going to happen next? (Is the recumbent woman on the extreme left about to *suckle* her companion?) If a splendid Rousseauesque lion were suddenly to wander through the drawing-room, we would scarcely bat an eyelid.

In that terminal ambiguity lies the extreme charm of Feuillade's pulp exoticism: i.e. because he had absolutely no intention to 'make strange', in the sense in which the phrase was employed by the Russian formalist critics (his sole ambition was to entertain his naïve and credulous audiences), the imagery of his films was rendered all the stranger.

The French avant-gardists of the period, Marcel L'Herbier to the fore, despised Feuillade, but the general public loved his work: not for the first time, the silent majority was out on a limb. And because he filmed his exteriors in natural décors, because he was also thereby a great documentarist, a poet of urban melancholy, recording the Paris of that curious transitional period, half nineteenth, half twentieth century, half *fin* and half *début de siècle,* which the Eiffel Tower appropriately bestrode and which in the cinema has been most eloquently commemorated by overhead railways, *art nouveau* Métro stations and similar nostalgic accessories of the Industrial Revolution, he reconciled Lumière and Méliès and led the cinema single-handedly out of its prehistory. Feuillade, good and true surrealist that he was, has always been by far the most *inexplicable* of filmmakers.

# 1919 Broken Blossoms

Lillian Gish was, above all else, a *face*. Hers was, so to speak, and is to this very day, the emblematic face of silent cinema, its spiritual radiance and near perfect symmetry of form enshrined for ever in the monochromatic oval portraiture of the iris dissolve that was so cherished by her mentor, D. W. Griffith.

In Griffith's early masterpieces, in a masterpiece like *Broken Blossoms,* the tale of the love of a lamblike Chinese for a waif of the Limehouse streets, the irredeemably dated contrived to coexist in paradoxical harmony with the, for the era in question, uncompromisingly up-to-date. On the one hand, these films (which also included *True Heart Susie, Way Down East* and *Orphans of the Storm*) were anchored, in strictly narrative terms, in the codes and conventions of Victorian melodrama, whether of the popular stage or the penny dreadful; on the other, they laid out once and for all the formal and technical parameters of an art form peculiar to the twentieth century. (By contrast with the stilted imagery of most of his contemporaries, imagery which constituted the uncanny visual equivalent of the language of silent film intertitles, Griffith's was so very lustrous one can scarcely credit that these films were ever *shot*.) As a performer, as almost a fetish, Gish wholly assumed and embodied that contradiction. The unmatched intensity with which she invested every role she played for Griffith – almost always that of a classic late-Victorian heroine, innocent, virginal and ripe for abuse – was never marred by any of the hysterical tics and tropes of her rivals. There was, in each of her performances, an emotional candour and simplicity which would permit her to continue acting into extreme old age (and most notably in Charles Laughton's *The Night of the Hunter,* a haunting fable in an unabashedly Griffithian tradition) without ever truly revising her style. At the same time, her soft, unfleshy, pre-Raphaelite features, demure yet not insipid, pale yet not spectral, beautiful yet without a trace of stereotyped Hollywood glamour, came to seem as indelibly 'Griffithian' as those of Jane Morris, for example, were indelibly 'Rossettian'.

Griffith's melodramas, though, unlike their theatrical or literary models, were seldom of an untempered sadistic or sadomasochistic trait. The pleasure which his public procured from them (and may, indeed, continue to procure from them) derived less from gloating over the seduction of a virginal young lass than from thrilling to her capacity for fighting her own corner, for defending herself, for surviving. The Griffithian heroine, of whom Gish has remained the archetype and the apotheosis, could also be spunky and humorous when occasion demanded; and if there ever existed a star whose legend did not require her, like Marilyn Monroe or James Dean, to suffer a premature death, it was she. She grew middle-aged, then elderly, then frankly old, precisely as one fancied the

characters whom she had played in the teens and twenties of the century might themselves have grown old. Her face, too, remained noble and dignified. It appeared neither a haggard wreck of its former self nor did it ever acquire the masklike waxiness of Hollywood's 'legion of the lifted'.

Lillian Gish was born in 1896, a mere ten months after Auguste and Louis Lumière organized the first public screening of images imprinted on celluloid. She died in 1993, just two years before the medium to which she dedicated her life celebrated its centenary. If, in the intervening decades, the world has all too often felt like cursing the very invention of the cinema, she at least, its guardian angel, never gave us cause to be anything but grateful.

# 1920 Das Kabinett des Dr Caligari
## *The Cabinet of Dr Caligari*

The distinction between denotations and connotations is one of the most basic in semiotics and may be applied to language at the most elementary level imaginable. Consider the sentence 'The cat sat on the mat'. What it *denotes* is, if you like, a charming little domestic tableau involving, exactly and literally (denotations are always literal), a cat sitting on a mat. On what might be called its *connotational* level, however, the message emitted belongs to a whole other contextual category. What this brief, elementary and monosyllabic configuration of words is clearly informing us is: 'I represent an example of sentence structure in an infant's first reading primer.' In short, if ever I should chance to see such a sentence, I think of neither cats nor mats but, instinctively, of just such a primer.

Similarly, with this characteristic illustration from *The Cabinet of Dr Caligari*. As it happens, I have seen Robert Wiene's film. Yet, when I look at the still, what I cannot help conjuring up in my inner eye is not, as is generally the case, an imploded impression, a compacted *flash*, of the film itself in its entirety but, curiously, a typical page out of a pre-war film history by Paul Rotha or Roger Manvell or Georges Sadoul in which this or else a comparable image from *Caligari* would invariably be found. Until the sixties, the fuzzy grey uniformity of most published photographic stills from the history of the cinema made it hard to distinguish decade from decade, let alone movie from movie. Bunched together on coarse, sandpapery, mustard-hued pages, frame enlargements from certified classics (*Alexander Nevsky, La Bête humaine* – ah, those railway tracks!) seemed to be coated with precisely the same ectoplasmic rust as other 'classics', so-called, which surely no one any longer wanted to see (Nicolai Ekk's *Road to Life,* Leopold Lindtberg's *Four in a Jeep,* umpteen humanist tracts from Emmer or Ermler). And, after about thirty years of regular exposure, more than a few such icons came to acquire the homey familiarity of snapshots in a previous generation's family album. If you clapped eyes once more on Stroheim's neck brace or Cherkassov's curling goatee (you felt his features, if inverted, would form a second, slightly less successful face, as in a Rex Whistler caricature), you would probably have thrown up over them.

Thus did *The Cabinet of Dr Caligari,* one of the world's most famous films, the Pavlovian response to any general knowledge query on 'Expressionism in the cinema', long eke out a spectral existence, half-alive, half-seen and only ever half-remembered, in obsolete film histories. Then, as film history itself was modernized, streamlined in the wake of the auteur theory, Wiene's film was no

longer remembered, merely commemorated – therefore, by an odd paradox, forgotten – and ceased to be very much more than a title. Everyone has heard of *The Cabinet of Dr Caligari;* but, as the years elapse, as generation of *cinéphile* succeeds generation of *cinéphile*, there remain fewer and fewer people who have actually seen it. I intend that to be read absolutely literally: fewer people now have seen the film than in 1925 or 1935 or 1945. It's the fate that befalls most films, to be sure, but *Caligari* is the example *par excellence* of what I would term a 'false classic'. (Others, generally of a vague 'humanist' ideology, are Milestone's *All Quiet on the Western Front*, G. W. Pabst's *Westfront 1918* and *Kameradschaft*, Jacques Feyder's *La Kermesse héroique*, Julien Duvivier's *Un carnet de bal*, René Clair's *A nous la liberté*, William Wellman's *The Ox-Bow Incident*, even, arguably, except in Britain, David Lean's *Brief Encounter*.)

Is *Caligari* still worth seeing? In its systematic use of stylised sets, warped camera angles and outrageously theatrical make-up, it was an impasse, a cul-de-sac; it was the road the cinema did not take. If it has had any subsequent influence, then it has been, very indirectly, on the work of those (relatively rare) filmmakers who appear to consider themselves superior to their chosen medium – a Peter Greenaway, for example, a man of undoubted intelligence but an artist whose brains, like Wiene's, have gone to his head.

53

# 1921 The Sheik

What is there to be said about Rudolph Valentino?

That he was born in Castellaneta in Italy in 1895, the year the cinema too was born, and christened Rodolfo Alfonzo Raffaele Pierre Philibert Guglielmi. That he begged on the streets of Paris and was, on more than one occasion, arrested by the New York police on suspicion of petty theft, even blackmail. That, when employed as a taxi dancer, he was rescued from incarceration in the Tombs, a notoriously squalid detention centre in the same city, by the arrestingly surnamed actress Alla Nazimova. That his first marriage – to another actress, Jean Acker – was never consummated. And that he was once alliteratively anathematized by an editorial in the *Chicago Tribune*: 'When will we be rid of all these effeminate youths, pomaded, powdered, bejeweled and bedizened in the image of Rudy – that painted pansy?'

Or else that he was the Nijinsky of the tango, a Nijinsky who was never to find his Diaghilev, never to meet the filmmaker who might have fashioned a setting worthy of such an exotic gem. That there was no one quite like him for whispering sweet, silent nothings into his heroines' ears or blowing languorous smoke rings as if out of his own smouldering insides. That, for the American cinema, he so definitively established the parameters of the so-called 'Latin lover', he would be imitated not only by such contemporaries as Ramon Novarro and Ricardo Cortez but by as subtle a performer of the sound period as Charles Boyer – that, indeed, a trace of his orchidaceous mannerisms lingers on in an actor like Antonio Banderas. And that, if he strikes us now as more than a little ludicrous, this can be attributed to the fact that physical comeliness dates even more rapidly than it ages. (Even Dorian Gray, who did not age, must have 'dated' and his physical type become demodé.)

As everyone knows, when Valentino died at the age of thirty-one (from a perforated ulcer), he became a greater star than ever – or rather, something greater still than a star, a cult. His funeral was a positive riot, with thousands of flamboyantly grieving women lining the streets; and, every year since, on the anniversary of his death, a mysterious lady (or, given that the ritual started in 1927, conceivably a relay of mysterious ladies) has silently come to lay a wreath on his tomb. It's absurd and it's tacky and it could happen only in Hollywood, but it's also a potent illustration of the eroticized mythopoeia that the cinema has always possessed. If sex is the shortest distance between the ridiculous and the sublime, then Valentino was simultaneously ridiculous *and* sublime. He was a real star – and real stars, no less than those in the sky, laugh at safety nets.

As for *The Sheik* (directed, for the record, by George Melford), it proved nearly as much of a sensation as its star's subsequent funeral. Droves of women

spectators swooned in the aisles and Arab motifs became a filmic fad for several years to come. So very successful was it, in fact, it spawned a sequel, Valentino's last film, *The Son of the Sheik*.

Was that the first time the 'Son of . . .' formula was used in the American cinema? Almost certainly not; but it was certainly the first to have permanently lodged itself in film history. Oh, those were innocent days, the days when sequels relied on codified formulae like 'Return of . . .' and 'Son of . . .' and 'Return of the Son of . . .'! Now, when one considers Hollywood's current mania for sequels and prequels, when one considers, too, how many of these new movies are not sequels at all, in the proper sense, but unashamed *clones* of the source material, one cannot help thinking that it might be more honest (and, for the type of spectator who looks to a sequel for security, probably a lot more enticing) to call the next episode in the *Rocky* cycle, for example, not *Rocky VI* but *Rocky Ditto*.

# 1922  La Femme de nulle part

## *The Woman from Nowhere*

I have never seen *La Femme de nulle part*. Not, I should say at once, that Louis Delluc's film belongs among the cinema's lost masterpieces: adequate prints of it still exist and my old alma mater in matters *ès-cinéma*, the Cinémathèque Française, used to screen it quite regularly. Nor is Delluc himself an unknown quantity. Better known now as a film critic than filmmaker (he died of tuberculosis at the age of thirty-three before properly consolidating his reputation as a director), he was one of the medium's earliest theorists, a theorist, moreover, whose (recently reprinted) writings continue to merit attention and close study. The Prix Delluc, the most prestigious award to be bestowed by the French film industry, was named after him.

No, if I have never seen *La Femme de nulle part,* it's because I have never wanted to see it, because, in effect, I have consciously avoided seeing it. And if I have consciously avoided seeing it, it's because I wanted to make absolutely certain that exposure to the film itself would not undermine my fascination with the image (a frame enlargement) reproduced opposite, the only image from *La Femme de nulle part* of which I have ever seen a reproduction, an image which has (perhaps more powerfully as a still shot than when inscribed within the evolving flux and flow of the film proper) long haunted the collective cinéphilic imagination. I know, from having read about the film, what its vaguely Pirandellian narrative involves: a middle-aged woman belatedly returns to the Italian villa that she once fled with her lover and contrives by her mere presence to deter the young married woman who presently occupies it (and who might be regarded as her own younger self) from committing the same error. I know, equally, that the central role was written for Eleanora Duse but was actually taken by the director's wife, Eve Francis, one of those exalted divas so cherished by the French avant-gardist school of the nineteen-twenties. And I know, finally (or have been led to believe), that although Delluc is frequently bracketed as a filmmaker with that avant-garde (which included Marcel L'Herbier, Abel Gance, Jean Epstein and Germaine Dulac, for whom Delluc wrote the script of *La Fête espagnole*), his film is sober, almost arid, in tone, devoid of the formal artifices that one tends to associate with the movement. As a *cinéphile*, I cannot help being so informed. Yet even that very partial information has already diminished for me the charm of this meaninglessly beautiful image of a woman, clearly a woman of the world, who has suddenly been transplanted onto a deserted country road (of a type that reappeared, its oneiric mystery intact, in a couple of the later films of Luis Buñuel, *La Voie lactée* and *Le Charme discret de*

*la bourgeoisie*), a road I like to think of as itself coming from nowhere and going nowhere.

And my fascination with the image, my indifference, almost my hostility, to the film which generated it, prompts me to pose one of the most germane questions which ever can be posed about the cinema: *Can one tell from a still alone whether a film is good?* One has so often seen a mouth-watering still from some little B-movie thriller of the thirties or forties, a still reverberating with purplish, pulpish poetry (a gangster caught in a pool of shadow with a revolver clutched in his hand; a woman, encased in furs and feathers like a Sioux chieftain, draped over an *art déco* divan), only to discover that the movie itself is almost entirely without distinction. If one could somehow, heroically, discipline oneself to watch such a movie exclusively as a collection of single images, an album of single images (which is of course impossible), it would indeed be a masterpiece; when one watches it (as one always does) at the codified speed of twenty-four frames a second, it turns out as often as not to be an utter nullity. That is, after all, why we call the thing a *motion* picture – the cinema is not a visual but a *kinetic* art.

And that is why I have never seen *La Femme de nulle part* nor ever wanted to see it. Nothing in its unfolding narrative could possibly be as haunting and haunted as this single arresting and arrested image.

# 1923 Our Hospitality

The distinctive virtue of this shot from *Our Hospitality* is that it is, as they say, *for real*. The cascade is a real cascade, and the man poised on its cusp, preparing to abseil to the rocks beneath, rocks on which a young maiden (a damsel, I'm almost tempted to call her) lies stretched out in a faint, is not a stunt man but the movie's star – Buster Keaton, needless to say. By definition, the whole astonishing sequence, just one of several of its kind in Keaton's cinema, would have to have been completed in a single take.

This is not an insignificant point. André Bazin, patron of the *nouvelle vague*, an admirer of Flaherty and Rossellini and a fervent apologist of the filmic 'real', of the inviolate integrity of the cinematic image, had absolutely nothing against fiction films, nothing against the cinema telling a story – but he took very violent exception to its telling a lie (to the reprocessing of a film in the laboratory, for example). In this sense, then, at the level of the shot if not of the narrative as a whole, *Our Hospitality* might be called Bazinian. On the one hand, its extravagant if hackneyed plot (concerning two feuding families in the American South) urgently demands that suspension of disbelief crucial to the fluent functioning of all illusionistic fictions; on the other hand, it's a flabbergasted suspension of *belief* that tends to be prompted by a sequence like the one illustrated above. We see it, and we still don't believe it. It is, nevertheless, for real.

Such a sequence, moreover, was not merely devised for some notional anthology of stunts but was exploited by Keaton as a *romantic* gambit. If his heroines appeared oddly passive (by contrast, certainly, with Chaplin's), it was because their function was above all to be *rescued*. The beautiful, spaniel-faced Keaton was the most chivalrous of clowns, for whom eleventh-hour rescues were as so many declarations of love. Where most movie heroes would plight their troth under the sort of dreamy, balmy moon that has immemorially rhymed with 'June', he was never more dashingly amorous than during a flood or a landslide.

The single fact that everyone knows about Keaton before even seeing any of his movies is, of course, that he never smiled. Which, if true enough as far as it goes, is a fact of little consequence to anyone genuinely conversant with his work. For if he did neither smile nor laugh on screen, his face was nevertheless amazingly expressive, as expressive as that of an animal, a dog, perhaps, which, although equally incapable of smiling or laughing, contrives quite affectingly to communicate its feelings. Keaton was the silent cinema's great dumb animal.

And that walk of his. He seemed to walk a few inches off the ground – or rather, to walk the tightrope *on* the ground, thereby, even when no imminently

looming danger threatened him, assuming something of the acrobat's prestige and grace. I myself smile when I think of that weird walk, that lonely, lovely, indomitable goose-step that would be transformed ever so gradually into a run as if by the winding of some big, invisible key in the small of his back. I smile when I think of Keaton, his straw boater sitting at a precise ninety-degree tangent to his head, being pursued through Hollywood's leafy, small-town streets by an ageless Mack Sennett dog with a perennial black eye. And I smile when I think of him being pursued by cyclones, tornadoes, hurricanes and, in *Seven Chances,* more terrifying than any of these, by scores of furious brides-to-be, by a regiment of women that also resembled a hurricane, one of those to which, as if coincidentally, the names of women used to be given.

Buster Keaton was a prince, an angel and, if I may bestow on him the highest title of honour that I know, an exception. Only the noblest music should accompany his films.

# 1924 Greed

It's the story told about *Greed,* rather than the story told by it, which has always been far the better known. Its mutilation has remained the American cinema's single most celebrated disgrace: the fact that what its director, Erich von Stroheim, initially delivered to Metro-Goldwyn-Mayer was a forty-two-reel adaptation of the Frank Norris novel *McTeague* – a film, then, whose running time would be around seven hours (by no means unheard-of today, of course); that, under pressure from the studio's self-styled 'genius-in-residence', the egregious Irving Thalberg, Stroheim himself agreed to 'trim' the footage back to twenty-four reels; that MGM then decided to take the film out of his hands and assigned Rex Ingram, the director of *The Four Horsemen of the Apocalypse,* hence not just anyone, to bring it in at a more manageable eighteen; that not even these swingeing cuts satisfied Thalberg, who finally released it at ten; and that the few insiders who saw Stroheim's own version claimed that it was one of the greatest films ever made. According to certain unverifiable sources, a complete print is preserved to this day in MGM's vaults. In view of the extraordinary mileage, however, both commercial and critical, to be gained by the revelation of such a treasure, this is rather hard to believe.

As an actor, Stroheim was popularly nicknamed 'the man you love to hate'. But, as a director, too, at least for the Hollywood establishment, that's exactly what he had always been. *Greed* was not the first of his films to have got him in trouble. For *Foolish Wives,* whose shoot lasted a year and whose budget eventually spiralled upward to a million dollars, a length of time and sum of money unprecedented for the twenties, he inveigled Universal into constructing a (reputedly) life-size replication of Monte-Carlo and insisted that the Austrian hussars who figure prominently in the film be outfitted with the regulation underwear beneath their uniforms! According to Ephraim Katz's *International Film Encyclopaedia,* moreover, 'In his quest for realism he spent days trying to film flying birds in just the right flight pattern.' *Foolish Wives,* although ultimately a commercial success, was also a near disaster for Universal, since its extravagantly bloated budget had reduced the studio's profit margin to next-to-nothing. How the moguls must have loved to hate Stroheim!

But reconsider Katz's phrase 'in his quest for realism'. Stroheim, every film historian will concur, was a realist, *Greed* one of the supreme realist dramas of human psychology, so much so as to be practically *aromatic.* Even his characters' never-to-be-seen underwear, we now know, was realistically in period. Look, though, at the still opposite. It depicts a wedding, that of Gibson Gowland, the bovine blond standing second from the left, to ZaSu Pitts, in the centre. Look, now, at Pitts herself. Who does she resemble? Who else but

Popeye's steady, long-suffering girlfriend, Olive Oyl. And the best man on her left (played by Jean Hersholt), with his nerve-rackingly pinstriped suit, his gaudy necktie and his Mickey Mouse gloves? Isn't he a dead ringer for the arch-villain Flattop in the *Dick Tracy* comic strip? And the infant in the left foreground? Couldn't he, too, have stepped out of some turn-of-the-century comic book, out of McCay's *Little Nemo,* for example, or maybe *The Katzenjammer Kids*?

Compare the whole image, finally, with another reproduced in this book, on page 105, the climactic family gathering from Frank Capra's *It's a Wonderful Life,* a film that no one has ever deigned to think of as 'realistic'. Another family gathering, as I say, another married couple, even another infant in the foreground. But which of the two images seems more rooted in the lifelike? Even if James Stewart and Donna Reed have a crumpled homespun glamour which few of us could honestly claim for ourselves, isn't it they who strike us as more closely approximating our own unidealized self-image? All of which raises an interesting issue (one which concerns not only Stroheim's work but that of such contemporary practitioners of filmic realism as Mike Leigh and Ken Loach, John Cassavetes and Maurice Pialat): to wit, just how realistic *is* realism? Could it be that ordinary people themselves, those people who comprise the stuff and matter of realism, filmic, literary or whatever, simply are not, and have never been, realistic? That realism is, effectively, the very opposite of the real?

# 1925 Bronenosets Potyomkin
## *The Battleship Potemkin*

The Odessa Steps sequence! Long have scholars sought to dispel what one might call the epistemological ambiguity at the core of the most famous sequence in *The Battleship Potemkin* (and arguably still the most famous strip of film in the world). Long have they been at pains to disengage the myth of the filmed event from the wholly distinct reality of the Kronstadt mutiny which inspired it, at pains to insist that Sergei Eisenstein reinvented history (his story?), that the Odessa Steps massacre never happened, that the Steps never existed, that there's no such place as Odessa (well, almost). It is, however, a lost cause. Goethe, despite not having seen the film, defined it best: 'The reverse of reality to obtain the height of truth.' And there was this from Cocteau: 'Alexandre Dumas, Michelet, Eisenstein, the only real historians.' He added: 'One of the countless qualities of *Potemkin* is to look as if it was shot by nobody, performed by nobody.'

Is it true, though? When I look at the image opposite, I cannot doubt that it was shot by somebody, that it was the product of an artist's vision. Life does not engender compositions so indelibly dynamic – or, should I say, it didn't in 1905, for if it sometimes does today, if news photographers do succeed from time to time in producing stunningly composed images, it's precisely by virtue of (among others) Eisenstein's prior example.

Actually, the word 'composition', equally a musical term after all, seems to me an appropriate one here. For what I see is not steps but musical staves; not the Tsarist soldiery and their butchered victims but an evenly sprinkled cluster of crotchets and quavers and semiquavers: all it needs to complete the illusion is the statutory treble clef in the extreme left-hand margin. And when I watch the sequence itself, as it unfolds on a cinema screen, it's almost as if I'm witnessing the alchemical transposition, into an exclusively visual medium, of the aural violence and dissonance of another Sergei, Prokofiev, the composer with whom Eisenstein was later to collaborate on *Alexander Nevsky* and *Ivan the Terrible*. *Potemkin* is, perhaps, a filmic cantata.

Such an analogy may strike the reader as merely a facile paradox, but I'm prepared, by switching metaphors, to go further. First, however, a little film history is in order. Although one could doubtless cite the odd exception, I think it true to say on general grounds that, where the sophistication of its discourse, and the individual elements of which that discourse was made up (narrative construction, psychological depth, technical innovation, and so forth), are concerned, the cinema took exactly thirty-six years to catch up with the other,

very much more ancient, art forms. It wasn't, I say, until Fritz Lang's *M* in 1931, an extraordinary dissection of the mindset of a serial killer, that the cinema produced a work of art *for which absolutely no excuses had to be made*. *M* was, in short, a film as beautiful, intelligent, mysterious, innovative, or what you will, as any work in any other medium of its time.

Ultimately, the comparison is meaningless but, if the cinema in its first forty years of existence had already produced a fair number of geniuses (Griffith, Feuillade, Stroheim, Chaplin, Murnau), all of these proved deficient in one way or another if subjected to the criteria of modernity routinely applied to the rival art forms of the same era – Griffith if compared to Joyce, Feuillade to Debussy, Stroheim to Picasso, and so on. Of all of them, in other words, and this is probably the most vertiginous paradox of *silent* cinema, it could be said that they belonged to the medium's pre-modern, folkloric, story-telling phase – its *oral* period. And that period, a period during which films resembled nothing so much as tales told around a fire, and which, I suggest, finally came to an end with *M*, found its absolute apotheosis in *The Battleship Potemkin*, an epic story of heroes and martyrs, of ships and steps, not unworthy of Homer. Indeed, considering its still flickering splendour, one might claim that *Potemkin* was unique in being both the story *and* the fire.

# 1926  Bardelys the Magnificent

What is intriguing about this still is that, although it patently belongs to what is usually referred to as a costume picture (the period, for the record, is the reign of Louis XIII), one nevertheless knows that the film in question was not just set but actually made in the past. One knows equally, if obscurely, that it's an image dating from the Old, not the New, Testament of Hollywood's history, from the silent era rather than that of the talkies. And, last, one knows, or at least one suspects, that it's a shot from a Metro-Goldwyn-Mayer movie.

These connoisseurial convictions can be attributed above all to a certain quality, perceptible in the shot, of demure sumptuousness, the quality, in short, that we associate with late-Victorian, almost Tennysonian, melodrama (the flowers, the candles, the clothes and coiffures, the heroine's pose, the hero's profile and the perfect arc of his outstretched arm), a configuration of props and prototypes that would be inconceivable in virtually any American movie made after the watershed of the Second World War. It is, however, just the kind of gracious, classy, tasteful and slightly moribund imagery in which MGM specialized in the nineteen-twenties, when its logo, Leo the Lion, had already begun to epitomize Hollywood in its entirety just as Hoover has come to epitomize the vacuum cleaner and Bic the ball-point pen.

Yet there is a difference in this particular case. Photographs, specifically movie stills, might be defined as 'verbless': what the photographer eliminates from his miniature encapsulation of life and movement is, precisely, the faculty of motion, the 'doing word', the verb, as it were. And, occasionally, as in this still from King Vidor's *Bardelys the Magnificent,* a swashbuckler starring John Gilbert and Eleanor Boardman (the director's then wife), the 'doing word' has been eliminated for good. *Bardelys the Magnificent* no longer exists. It's a lost film. All that now remains of it is just this kind of posed snapshot, transfixing movement that can never again be cranked into life. (Quoting from himself, though, Vidor did insert a brief extract from the film in his still extant satire on Hollywood mores, *Show People.*)

It might be interesting to write a *parallel* history of Hollywood, articulated exclusively around those films which were mooted but, for one reason or another, never made. (The most regrettable of which would be Albert Lewin's projected adaptation of *The Picture of Dorian Gray* with Greta Garbo, no less, in the leading role, a project foredoomed by the actress's categorical refusal to re-emerge from retirement.) Interesting, too, to write a history of the American cinema as a chronicle, exclusively, of its lost films. These would include innumerable silent shorts by Griffith, Thomas Ince and John Ford, F. W. Murnau's *Four Devils* (like *Bardelys,* clinging to life only by a handful of still

shots), Mauritz Stiller's *The Street of Sin*, Ernst Lubitsch's *The Patriot*, Howard Hawks' *Air Circus*, Tod Browning's *London After Midnight*, Victor Seastrom's (or Sjöström's) *Tower of Lies* and Josef von Sternberg's *The Dragnet, The Case of Lena Smith* and of course *The Sea Gull*, which was both produced and, apparently, destroyed by Chaplin. Films unseen . . . as Keats might have put it.

Our image from *Bardelys* is more persuasive, probably, than was likely to have been the film which it illustrates. (Vidor, the director of *The Big Parade, The Crowd, Hallelujah, Our Daily Bread, Duel in the Sun* and a delirious adaptation of Ayn Rand's novel *The Fountainhead*, was perhaps not ideally suited to gorgeously upholstered costume dramas.) But it's not only for that reason that I cannot quite regret its disappearance. There's something strangely poignant about the whole notion of a 'lost' film, about the notion that a medium as slick and sleek and streamlined as the cinema turns out all along to have been as vulnerable as other, very much older and more artisanal art forms. That a painting can be lost, yes, naturally, or an illuminated manuscript, or a score by Bach or Monteverdi, or even the choreography of a great nineteenth-century Russian ballet that no one knew properly how to transcribe. But a film? A *movie*, for God's sake? I find something perversely thrilling, something oddly *ennobling*, in such a loss.

# 1927 Sunrise

1927. For a true *cinéphile* 1927 was the year not of the advent of the talkies but of the apogee of the silents, the year not of *The Jazz Singer,* which has secured its enduring niche in the cinema's history less because it was the finest of anything than solely because it was the first of something, but of F. W. Murnau's *Sunrise,* perhaps the most exquisitely beautiful film in the world.

1995. In 1995 only an idiot would venture to contain a definition of the cinema within a single lapidary formula. One is tempted, nevertheless, to speculate that the medium's chromosomal essence – its DNA, so to speak – must reside in the tension generated between what is filmed and what is not filmed. The camera describes a lateral pan, let's say, closely tracking the movement of a performer through an interior: that is what *is* filmed. As the pan proceeds, however, a set of visual units within the frame (a window, a vase, a painting, perhaps another character in the same room) will necessarily 'pan' in the reverse direction, meeting, then being obscured by, then subsequently reappearing behind the figure in the foreground: that is what is *not* filmed (which is to say, the effect of these shifting units on the plasticity of the basic composition can never be completely premeditated). Although certain directors (Sternberg, Resnais, Fellini, the Eisenstein of *Ivan the Terrible*) did indeed endeavour to gain maximal control over the internal organization of their material, the sole instance of total, even totalitarian, domination that comes to mind is *Sunrise.*

Consider, from the film, an early scene in which Janet Gaynor, having prepared a lunch box, waits under a tree for her husband, George O'Brien, who is at that moment ploughing his little tract of land. The ox harnessed to the plough enters the frame diagonally from the lower right-hand corner, advances just far enough for the preordained image to fall exactly into place . . . and comes to an abrupt halt. Had that ox advanced a fraction of an inch more, the whole composition would have gone askew. Or, again, consider the image which graces the page opposite, consider the angle of the skiff, of its crossway seat, of the watered-silk quiver of reflections on the surface of what is unmistakably a studio tank – a single ill-judged detail, again, as I say, would have fatally compromised its painterly perfection. In this, at least, Murnau approached that impossible, unthinkable ideal: the cinema's Vermeer.

But what precisely was *Sunrise?* With Vidor's *The Crowd* and Paul Fejos' *Lonesome* (whose titles, not coincidentally, encapsulate the two sociomythic polarities of all contemporary urban alienation), it was one of the supreme masterpieces of a genre that might be dubbed, with a nod to Dreiser, the 'American tragedy'. No names, generally, were accorded the young protagonists of this genre, who, less characters than definitions, remained the Boy and the

Girl throughout. Nor was the metropolis in which they met, fell in love and lost one another referred to as anything but the Big City. Neither wholly American nor wholly German, this Big City was a honeycombed hive of damp tenements and humid beaches, of bars, barber shops and barber-shop quartets. And its traditional playground was what used to be called a Luna-Park, a vast machine of pleasure and pain through which our heroes were pulled, pushed, squeezed and wrung, like Chaplin in the factory of *Modern Times*.

Vidor and Fejos were primitives, however; Murnau, the cinema's most sophisticated artist. In the Big City of *Sunrise* there is an El, an overhead railway, which constitutes in and of itself a lesson in pure *mise-en-scène*. For we now know that, in order to create an illusion of perspective comparable to that formulated by the painters of the quattrocento and in order, yet again, to affirm his absolute mastery of every single element on the screen, Murnau had a train constructed that was composed of decreasingly small compartments, the first of them occupied by adults, the following ones by midgets, the last of all by dolls. Thus, in his uncompromising conception of the cinema, the solution to a mystery would become a mystery in its turn, the very mechanics of poetry would be enhaloed by poetry.

# 1928 Chelovek s kinoapparatom
## *The Man with a Movie Camera*

What would be the motto of Dziga Vertov's *The Man with a Movie Camera*? I am a camera? The eye is a camera? The camera is an eye? The camera is an I? The eye is an I?

'Dziga Vertov' was in fact a pseudonym, signifying 'spinning top' in Russian: the director of *The Man with a Movie Camera* was born Denis Abramovich Kaufman. (His two brothers were Mikhail Kaufman, a celebrated Soviet documentarist, and Boris Kaufman, the cinematographer of all four of Jean Vigo's films, of Elia Kazan's *On the Waterfront* and Sidney Lumet's *The Group*, among others.) In 1919, with an odd assortment of like-minded young filmmakers, Vertov founded an avant-garde group which he named the 'kinoki', or the 'kinoks', or the 'cinema-eyes', and declared the primacy of the film camera, or 'Kino-Eye', over the human eye. To one of his first feature films, in addition, he gave the title *Kino-Glaz*, or, as it would be known in English, *Cinema-Eye – Life Caught Unawares*.

Yet Vertov was not a 'camera', not merely the passive recording agent suggested by Isherwood's famous four-word manifesto – since, with the ingenuity of a card sharper, he would deploy every conceivable *trompe-l'oeil* device available to filmmakers of the period: slow, speeded-up and reverse motion, split screen, multiple superimpositions, animation, still photography, even constructivist graphics. Nor was he just an 'eye', as one might designate some brilliant visual pictorialist like Lean or Wenders – since he never ceased to believe in the virtues of 'dialectical montage', in the now rather obsolete notion that the significance of a cinematic image derives less from its own discrete context than from its contextual relationship with the images that directly precede and follow it, derives, therefore, from that part of a filmic continuity that by definition *cannot* be seen. And, finally, he struggled long and hard not to be complacently an 'I', which is to say, an auteur filtering his filmic material through a personal style, through a set of individualistic mannerisms as indelibly stamped on his imagery as a watermark – since, right up to his death in 1954, he continued to defend a Stalinistico-utopian vision of the mass as the sole vehicle of meaning and change in society (a struggle that, since he was a great artist, would prove utterly vain).

It would probably be fair to say that Vertov's work is regarded nowadays as more of an influence on other filmmakers than as a living creation to be seen, admired and reflected on for its own sake. As the film portrait of a contemporary city (actually, an amalgam of Moscow, Kiev and Odessa), the tessellated

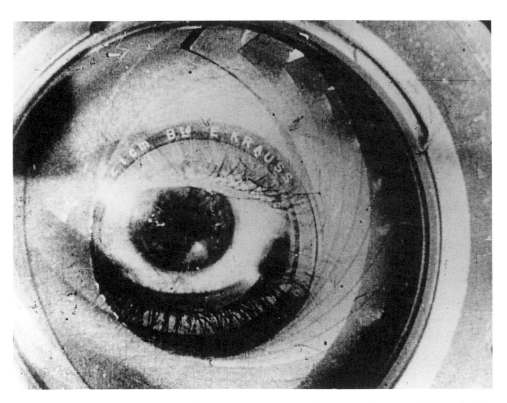

fragmentation of *The Man with a Movie Camera,* for example, would launch the whole mode of 'city symphonies', documentaries whose dawn-to-dusk chronology endeavoured to distil the textural essence of a given metropolis (Paris for Alberto Cavalcanti, Berlin for Walter Ruttmann, and so on) through kinetic montages of criss-crossing tramlines, youthful, sun-dappled cyclists and rhythmically juxtaposed neon signs. A trace of his segmentally lyrical purchase on reality can also be detected in the films of artists as ideologically opposed as Humphrey Jennings and Leni Riefenstahl (whose athletes, in *Olympia,* would create their own, natural slow and speeded-up motion). And the most important element of his experimentation, the way in which his imagery would regularly confront the spectator with the source of its relentlessly unfolding skein, the camera-eye, became almost a cliché in the work of Chris Marker, Michael Snow and Jean-Luc Godard (who named after Vertov the militant group of filmmakers which he founded with Jean-Pierre Gorin in the wake of May 1968).

In one sense Vertov failed. Hoping to remove, in a single sweep, the cinema's illusionistic undertow was like attempting to yank a tablecloth from off a table set for dinner without disturbing any of the dishes or cutlery. In another sense, though (even if it's a sense which he himself would not have acknowledged), he succeeded. He achieved, after all, what Cyril Connolly once declared was the ultimate, defining duty of all artists, whatever their ideological allegiances: he produced a masterpiece.

# 1929 L'Argent
## *Money*

In a preliminary note to the designer Tony Walton, who was about to fashion the costumes of *Fahrenheit 451,* François Truffaut wrote the following: 'Speaking of glossy materials, I have always thought that Carole Lombard's gown in *To Be or Not to Be* is the most erotic woman's costume ever to have been seen in the cinema.'

I beg to differ. I would counterpropose the gown (and hat, and furs, and accessories) worn by Brigitte Helm in *L'Argent. L'Argent* (or *Money*), directed by Marcel L'Herbier, a modernized adaptation of Zola's novel of the Parisian stock exchange (and hence no relation to Robert Bresson's *L'Argent,* made more than a half-century later and loosely based on a novella by Tolstoy), is one of the neglected masterpieces of film history, unforgettable in its visual glitter and formal complexity. To any interested reader I would recommend (a) attempting to see it, of course (not an easy task, although it was superbly restored in the late seventies), and (b) reading the brilliant monograph on L'Herbier by a Paris-based, American-born film critic and theorist, Noël Burch. What concerns me here, though, is not the film itself but this heavenly vision of Helm (an actress more familiar as the robot Maria in Lang's *Metropolis* and still alive today, at the age of eighty-nine) with her sharp-nosed profile and strange, columbaceous neck, the neck of one of Ingres's naked, virginally orificeless odalisques, and above all with those furs, that hat, that gown.

Somewhere else in the same collection of letters Truffaut quotes this aphorism by the film historian George Jean Auriol: 'The cinema consists in having beautiful things done to beautiful women.' Times *have* changed. Who, currently, would dare to define the cinema in such flagrantly sexist language? Who, currently, would dare to equate in so unrepentant a manner the two concepts of 'femininity' and 'beauty', as if the latter were the sole ideal to which the former should aspire? And who, currently, would be caught rhapsodizing on the prospect of 'doing' things to women (no matter how 'beautiful'), with its unformulated but, to our perhaps hypersensitive ears, also unmissable implication of rape. Yet the history of the medium *is* equally a history of beautiful women; and such is the privilege and power of feminine beauty, or even the memory of that beauty, it's not surprising that admirers like Christopher Isherwood and Kenneth Tynan paid court to Louise Brooks at the very end of her life simply because she had *once* been beautiful and had *once* been in the movies.

For it's through the camera's lens, as it caresses the objects of our fantasies,

that we come to understand how bodies and faces, no less than the clothing and cosmetics that are worn by them, have always been subject to the dictates of cinematic fashion. From one decade to the next, legs have grown longer and slimmer, as skirts have. Busts have become more or less generous, and blouses have followed suit. To and fro, year by year, the pendulum has swung, and the great designers of face and form, the Balenciagas and Sternbergs, the Diors and Cukors, the Saint-Laurents and Truffauts, the Gaultiers and Beneixes, have unveiled their latest collections and sent their supermodels parading down the catwalk of the screen – from Clara Bow, the flapper personified, of the head-lamp eyes and pouty bee-sting lips, to Carole Lombard, in whom droll spoilt-child petulance somehow contrived to cohabit with incomparably glamorous poise and self-assurance, from Greta Garbo, the Mona Lisa of Hollywood's Louvre, to Marilyn Monroe, its Victoire de Samothrace, from Gina Lollobrigida, whose sexiness was that of a rather dated striptease act, the stripper herself remaining comically aloof from anything taking place further down her body, to Nastassja Kinski, whose frail and eerie presence was infused by the very qualities that her name so felicitously evoked, the nostalgic and the kinky.

Politically incorrect it may well be to glory in it, but the cinema is still, as it has always been, a Mount Rushmore of feminine faces and bodies – faces and bodies over whose giant sculpted features I would love to scramble, like Cary Grant and Eva Marie Saint at the climax of *North By Northwest.*

# 1930 Other Men's Women

There was, perhaps, nothing ineluctable about the cinema's passage from silence to sound, and it's even possible to postulate an alternative history of film, one in which sound, dismissed as a mere gimmick, would have proved of no more enduring value than 3-D. It's worth recalling, nevertheless, that in the ebbing years of silence (and the movies were like children: they didn't all start talking at the same time) there emerged not only a few of the medium's supreme masterworks but scores of stagy featurettes which, so to say, positively cried out for sound, paradoxically 'wordy' dramas whose meaning was conveyed less by their imagery than by the intertitles that punctuated it. They were talkies before talkies had been invented, and the advent of sound only accentuated their endemic theatricality.

Then there was William Wellman's *Other Men's Women,* not just the first indisputably great sound film but one of the greatest ever made in Hollywood. *Other Men's Women*? Who, you ask, has heard of *Other Men's Women*? Which is another reason for being grateful to this amazing film: the conclusive manner in which its scandalous neglect has confirmed, if confirmation were needed, that a genuine discovery, a *revelation,* is still possible in a medium as raked over, as obsessively pawed over, as the cinema.

In effect, our appreciation of the classic Hollywood product has been as influenced by the tastes of the Young Turks of French film criticism as their own subsequent films were influenced by the masters whom they adulated. But although those masters, Hitchcock, Hawks, Ray, Mann, Welles, Sternberg and Co., continue to this day to personify, in film histories and analyses, Hollywood at its finest, it should be pointed out that the testing sample from which their champions evolved a whole new theory of the American cinema (the so-called auteur theory) was a biased and incomplete one, based as it was on what was available to them in a given place (Paris) and at a given time (the fifties). Now, with the expanding circulation of old movies on television and video, we can see just how fallible they were. Errors were frequent, omissions even more so. And one such omission was *Other Men's Women.*

Two men, friends from way back, work on the railroad together. One of them (Grant Withers) is an overgrown adolescent, a carefree player of the field, the other (Regis Toomey) a contentedly married man with a wife quite a bit younger than he (Mary Astor). Withers is invited to move into his friend's modest little bungalow; inevitably, he and Astor fall in love; a love which will bring blindness and death in its wake.

It's an artless, almost naïve tale, as apparently artless and naïve as certain films by Renoir: it recalls *La Bête humaine* (for its evocatively filmed, often nocturnal, railroad scenes), but also *La Chienne* (for its obscurely, if in this instance chastely,

pornographic atmosphere). One thinks, equally, of Jean Vigo's *L'Atalante,* for the breathtaking narrative liberties that Wellman takes: Withers, leaving his freight train completely untended to snatch a ham-and-egg breakfast in a trackside diner and watching a seemingly endless chain of coaches shunt past the window behind him; a youthful James Cagney entering a dance hall and suddenly, by himself, and with utter disregard for narrative plausibility, letting rip with a virtuoso tap routine (in a scene which anticipates the early *nouvelle vague* in general and Godard's *Bande à part* in particular); an elderly, one-legged man using his peg leg to punch a row of holes in the earth for Mary Astor to plant seeds in her bungalow garden. Scene by scene, even shot by shot, *Other Men's Women* is something of a miracle – and although not unaffecting in its sober beauty, the accompanying illustration, one of the very few available for reproduction, entirely fails to do justice to its grace and invention.

The French 'chef-d'oeuvre' and the English 'masterpiece' are, of course, exact synonyms. Within the tight little world of film studies, though, and given the systematic inflation of values which marked the original formulation of the auteur theory, coupled with a chronic Anglo-American reluctance to be generous with superlatives, there have always been substantially more *chef-d'oeuvres* than masterpieces in the cinema. Yet another reason, then, for treasuring *Other Men's Women* is that it is a genuine masterpiece but, by virtue of French neglect, not (or not yet) a *chef-d'oeuvre.*

# 1931 Freaks

There exist 'facts of cinema' as there exist 'facts of life', and one of these facts, specifically distinguishing the cinema from life, is that, on the screen, physical and in particular facial beauty constitutes the *norm*. (The assertion is more applicable to the American cinema than to those of Europe and the Third World, but it's a near axiom nevertheless). In life, as we know, on occasion to our emotional cost, physical beauty necessarily 'signifies': it alters our perception of, and our relationship to, the person who is fortunate enough to possess it. In the cinema, by contrast, such beauty is almost never significant in itself; if unaided, it is, in other words, an insufficient condition for the generating of a fiction. In Clarence Badger's silent comedy *It,* for example, Clara Bow plays a coquettish shop-girl who, in spite of her (in reality) exquisite appearance, is connoted in the plot as being merely, averagely 'pretty', a *banalization* of physical beauty that is no more than par for the Hollywood course. It is, in consequence, ugliness that has always tended to be the more effective conductor of filmic narrative, whether in the vein of science-fiction (James Whale's *Frankenstein*), Gothic horror (Tod Browning's *Dracula*), Grand Guignol (Robert Aldrich's *Whatever Happened to Baby Jane?*) or the 'compassionate' case-history (David Lynch's *The Elephant Man*).

Ugliness was invented for the cinema by Lon Chaney in 1925 – it was he who first, in a single shot, established the attraction/repulsion bind which has remained its governing parameter ever since. The shot in question occurs in Rupert Julian's adaptation of *The Phantom of the Opera*. The disfigured Phantom, played by Chaney, has sequestered the virginal object of his infatuation, a young soprano, in his well-appointed sanctum underneath the stage of the Paris Opéra and is finally about to consummate his festering desire. The gesture which he proceeds to make towards her, however, seems to intimate no more than the vague wish to caress her shoulder; even so, already conscious of the spectacle of physical deformity which he must offer her, he is unable to prevent himself, before he quite manages to make contact, from arresting his gesture in mid-movement and nervously withdrawing his arm. In that instant of infinitely affecting hesitation – between the Phantom's morbid compulsion to exploit, and his human, all too human reluctance to soil, the delicacy which attracted him in the first place – resides the essence of most subsequent representations of physical ugliness on the screen.

In the silent era, of course, Chaney worked frequently with Tod Browning, and it was the mysterious, still underrated (indeed, still unknown) Browning who, with his extraordinary *Freaks*, drove a stake through the whole sickly pathos of cinematic ugliness. *Freaks,* to put it bluntly, is peopled by the sort of

figures whom one would not normally care to encounter in the dark night of a cinema auditorium, peopled, in short, by midgets, dwarfs, pinheads, bearded ladies and one particularly haunting armless and legless yet living being – all of them completely authentic. It belongs to a sinister tradition of films about the circus, sweaty films about *being tired of the circus,* smelly films about *detesting the circus,* from Sjöström's *He Who Gets Slapped* (featuring Chaney again) to Sternberg's *The Blue Angel,* from Ingmar Bergman's *Sawdust and Tinsel* to Elia Kazan's interesting, now forgotten *Man on a Tightrope.* It was, unbelievably, produced at MGM, Hollywood's lush and glamorous centre-court, the studio of Irving Thalberg and Louis B. Mayer, of *ars gratia artis* and entertainment as homey and American as Mom's apple pie, the studio, only a few years hence, of Mickey Rooney and Judy Garland, who would become the Peter Pan and Wendy of Hollywood's Neverland. It caused a furore on its brief initial release (one woman ran screaming from a San Diego preview cinema), was withdrawn from circulation for nearly three decades and has almost never been screened on television. It is, very precisely, the American cinema's *L'Age d'or.*

But just how good is it? There's the paradox. *Freaks* is a *beautiful* film. A film without compassion, but one also without condescension. A film which reminds us, too, that it was the Medusa's *beauty,* rather than her mythical ugliness, that petrified all who looked upon her.

75

# 1932 Trouble in Paradise

'It must be the most marvellous supper. We may not eat it, but it must be marvellous.' Thus Herbert Marshall, preparing an intimate *tête-à-tête*, to a Venetian *maître d'hôtel* in the opening scene of Ernst Lubitsch's *Trouble in Paradise*. He continues: 'And, waiter, you see that moon? I want to see that moon in the champagne.' (The waiter conscientiously scribbles on his notepad: 'Moon in champagne'.) 'As for you, waiter,' Marshall concludes, 'I don't want to see you at all.'

Whatever else are its claims on our attention, *Trouble in Paradise* is a masterpiece of *delivery,* the most mellifluous, the most perfectly *spoken,* film in the history of the American cinema. For just as Herbert Marshall looks, in his double-breasted suit, the way other men do only in white tie and tails, so the film's dialogue (by Samson Raphaelson and Grover Jones) charms the ear the way only poetry is supposed to do, and is given voice to by Marshall, by Kay Francis (with whom he is seen opposite), by Miriam Hopkins, Sir C. Aubrey Smith, Edward Everett Horton and Charlie Ruggles, as if it were the most brilliant light verse imaginable. Indeed, if there is a work of art to which it bears more than a superficial resemblance, it's not a film at all but a poem, *The Rape of the Lock.* So confident was Lubitsch that the rarefied featheriness of his comedy would withstand any shock to its system, he actually allowed the interpolation of a brief scene involving an anarchist (along with a reference to the Depression, an event which is, of course, rigorously excluded from the narrative proper), rather in the manner of the famous Hogarthian couplet of Pope's mock-epic:

> The hungry Judges soon the Sentence sign,
> And Wretches hang that Jury-Men may dine.

There exists a Lubitsch mythology. His films, so the argument runs, were enjoyable bijou fluff, set (as also were those of Clair, Mamoulian and Wilder) in a Europe as inconsequential as Monte-Carlo, a Ruritanian Europe, a quaintly transnational, transcultural and above all translingual principality. The capital of this Hollywoodized Europe, and the epitome of Continental sophistication, was Paris – Paris, Paramount – a Paris whose trademark was the Eiffel Tower, a Paris in which one took champagne as in Baden-Baden one takes the waters, a Paris in which Garbo (in Lubitsch's *Ninotchka*) bought a preposterous hat that would then sit perched on her head at the exact angle of a slipper out of which champagne is being drunk, a Paris in which peasant, butler and count, not to mention American heiress and White Russian taxi driver, mingled as casually as the beasts in one of those zoologically indiscriminate tableaux by the Douanier Rousseau.

Yet Jean-Marie Straub, an unlikely bedfellow, is on record as rating Lubitsch the equal of Murnau and Lang, and one would hardly expect Straub to be sensitive to so frivolous an iconography. What is it, then, that he finds to admire in him? Paradoxically, the height of cinematic abstraction. Or, then again, not so paradoxically, for Lubitsch *was* an abstract artist, a formalist, whose films (*Trouble in Paradise* in particular) were articulated through the deployment of a series of classical rhetorical figures – ellipsis, supremely, the trope of the so-called 'Lubitsch touch', the cunning art of conveying without actually showing, but also metaphor, metonymy, euphemism, litotes, and so forth. As such, *Trouble in Paradise* is as much a textbook inventory of filmic devices as *Citizen Kane*.

And the still? I chose it because I like it. I like its *art déco* severity. I like its epigrammatic economy. I like the clock. I like the clock *a lot*. I like those two profiles whose interstitial 'negative' space (that, in short, which separates one from the other) seems to form a spectral glass goblet, as in the sort of optical puzzle so beloved of vulgarizing mathematicians. And I would like to raise that spectral goblet and propose a toast to the memory of Ernst Lubitsch.

# 1933 Footlight Parade

Busby Berkeley! So many flowers, so many flower petals, so many flower maids, so many flowers made out of so many maids, so many maids made out of so many flowers, so many maids in a row, so many nudes, so many gilded staircases, so many nudes descending so many gilded staircases, so many fountains, so much rain, and inside each drop of rain another young woman arrests its fall by lasciviously opening an umbrella, so many umbrellas, a positive shower of umbrellas, those big black flowers whose petals open in the rain, so many revolving water lilies, so many exploding stars, so many exquisitely garlanded wheels on which the Grand Inquisitor, the veritable Torquemada, of dancing masters would break so many scantily attired butterflies!

But, of all the many torments which these butterflies had to endure, the most terrible must have been gradually to comprehend that this sadistic, Kafkaesque machine to which they were bound hand and foot was intended to reveal itself solely to a bird's-eye view or else to the atrocious, unblinking eye (like the cold, lashless eye of the camera itself) of a martinet heartlessly choreographing their gestures of flailing helplessness as they gaily screamed for mercy.

In the cinema Berkeley belonged to that select and eclectic subdivision of artists who, if genuine visual innovators, were nevertheless not, or not primarily, directors (Stefan Vorkapich, the deviser of filmic montages; Val Lewton, the creative producer of subtle horror; Saul Bass, the designer of brilliant credit-title sequences; Natalie Kalmus, Technicolor consultant on scores of gaudily beautiful films); and, if Hollywood was a Dream Factory, as the cliché has it, then what almost any one of his numbers represented was the Factory's automated assembly line.

It should be said, however, that the close if too often frivolous critical attention accorded Berkeley's work in recent years has tended to focus excessively on those overhead, pattern-making, neo-Futurist symmetries of his at the expense of some prodigious tracking, panning and dollying camera shots that ceaselessly redefine the spatial parameters of his vast, silvery, disklike sets before our dazed and dazzled eyes. Yet what is so uniquely bizarre about his Catherine Wheel formations is that, although usually rationalized in their narrative context as forming an integral part of the Broadway revue on whose triumphant, indeed orgasmic, opening night the whole plot is converging, the fact that they are filmed from directly overhead means that they must necessarily remain *invisible* to the theatre audience for whose benefit the film would have us believe they are being staged. That audience's view of the spectacle would be as partial and problematic as that of a visitor to an art gallery confronted with one of those horizontally or near-horizontally positioned paintings or maps seen in

certain works of *trompe l'oeil* and whose anamorphous perspectives can be corrected only by the application of a deforming lens. In Berkeley's case the deforming lens was the camera.

He was, therefore, an improbable descendant of his eighteenth-century namesake, the Bishop George Berkeley, famous for having posed, in *The Principles of Human Knowledge,* the conundrum of unperceived existence, the conundrum of what may be said to happen to a material object when it's no longer under human observation. Neither man, fortunately, was content to leave it at that. Each delivered the world *in extremis* from the spiritual nausea of solipsism: Berkeley the philosopher by hypothesizing the all-embracing vision of God; and Berkeley the choreographer by granting the spectator a Godlike overview of his *impossible stage.*

# 1934 The Scarlet Empress

Narcissus unfaithful to himself, Josef von Sternberg was a mad, Hoffmannesque goldsmith much of whose professional life was devoted to the creation of ever more ornate settings for a living jewel. He was an artist whose work, so haughty, so autocratic, so narcissistic, so utterly indifferent to the stylistic codes and conventions of the period to which it was supposed to belong, also constituted an obeisant, even masochistically servile, homage to the actress Marlene Dietrich. So much so that *The Shanghai Gesture,* in which she does not appear, and which was made after their collaboration had come to an end, was nevertheless imbued with her aura, her aroma, her perfume.

Following the triumph of *The Blue Angel,* they made six films together, six sumptuous masterpieces of romantic flummery, whose relation to the conventional wisdom of realism was precisely that of a parade of Mardi Gras carnival floats, six ostensibly novelettish fictions which have aged as little as did, at least during her public career, their star. In the rococo *Morocco* Dietrich, dressed in mannish tails, kissed a flustered young woman full on the lips and sashayed off into the Sahara as nonchalantly as if it were the *plage* at Deauville. In *Dishonored* she was cast as a fifth columnist whose Machiavellian machinations led her to a firing squad of lovelorn young *poilus* who could hardly bear to raise their rifles against her. In *Shanghai Express* she played a languorously orchidaceous sleeping-car Madonna. ('It took more than one man to change my name to Shanghai Lily.') In *Blonde Venus* she short-circuited the history of evolution (of which she herself could be considered the ideal culmination) by making her very first appearance clad from head to toe in a gorilla suit from which she then slinkily emerged. In *The Scarlet Empress* she impersonated a half-Firbankian, half-Eisensteinian (but Eisenstein hadn't yet made *Ivan the Terrible*) Catherine of Russia, a pack of silver wolfhounds snapping at her heels. And, in their final collaboration, *The Devil is a Woman,* her beauty had become so monstrously stylized, had been rendered so inhumanly abstract by the visual lacery, tracery and filigree on which her director doted, that if one had encountered her in the street one would have crossed oneself and fled in terror. It's a journalistic commonplace to compare her relationship with Sternberg to that of Pygmalion and Galatea, but Marlene's Pygmalion, as a sculptor, was closer to Epstein than to Maillol.

Sculptor he was, nevertheless, a sculptor in light and shade, a sculptor of holograms. But a sculptor – and this was his singularity as a filmmaker – whose work *melted* even as we contemplated it. Look at how everything in the image opposite, the candles, the pillars, the statues, even the boots that Marlene clutches in her hand and the fur lining of her gown, everything seems

deliquescent, seems about to liquefy, everything, that is, save her own serene presence, so innocent, so unexpectedly chaste, amid such outré putrefaction.

The aesthetic is that, weirdly in 1934, of the silent cinema, the cinema of light and shade, of sculpted forms that appear to melt into one another through the slow dissolves that have ever after been associated with Sternberg. And that, perhaps, is the ultimate paradox of his work. His pre-1929 movies, *Underworld*, for example, and *The Docks of New York*, were not so much silents as *talkies without sound*, in urgent need of an audio support that had not yet been invented or perfected. Watching them, one has the impression that one has suddenly gone deaf, a heretical comment to make of real silent films, whose silence does not detract from, but actually contrives to enhance, the filmic experience. *The Scarlet Empress*, by contrast, is a silent film with dialogue – the film, more accurately, *of a deaf man*, deaf to all the fads and fashions to which lesser directors are eternally in thrall.

# 1935 Becky Sharp

The cinema, it should be understood, was never what is called colour blind: it was, for the first forty years of its existence, almost entirely in black-and-white, a different matter altogether. Functioning, in a sense, as the very 'silence' of colour, the subtle monochrome cinematography typical of the twenties and thirties was, until it was gradually replaced, as little of a sensual deprivation as silence itself. For certain purists, indeed, the transposition from the near-absolute norm of black-and-white cinematography to the now absolute norm of colour remains one of the tragedies of the medium's history. Film, they feel, by definition, *is* in black-and-white. And, with the current ubiquity of colour, they feel, too, that movie studios have degenerated into beauty parlours, the movies themselves cosmeticized, not photographed, as thickly made-up as the stars who appear in them. For these purists, then, Rouben Mamoulian's *Becky Sharp,* a vulgar but not unamusing adaptation of Thackeray's *Vanity Fair,* and of historical significance as the first fully operative Technicolor feature, was a black day for the cinema.

I referred, though, to a 'near-absolute' norm of black-and-white. In effect, the colour cinema is practically as old as the cinema itself. By the turn of the century film stock was routinely tinted (the first-person gunshot of *The Great Train Robbery* was originally shown in a bright, brash, sanguinary red); and, by 1906, the British pioneering filmmaker George Albert Smith had patented his two-tone colour system, Kinemacolour. (The two tones were orangey red and blueish green.) Technicolor, the process of *Becky Sharp,* dates from 1915, and two-tone Technicolor (the same two stop-and-go tones as Kinemacolour) was regularly employed during the twenties and thirties. Who could ever forget, in *The Black Pirate,* for example (an uningratiatingly titled film under the circumstances), the two-tone spectacle of Douglas Fairbanks, resplendent in striped crimson pants, silver dripping from his ears, swinging from the rigging of his ship right up on to the screen itself, so close to it, in any event, that he seemed about to jump through it as through a paper hoop and land among us in the auditorium, breathless but still upright? And who could honestly swear, hand on heart, that he would have preferred such a spectacle to have been in black-and-white?

Certainly, for someone as myopic as I myself am, it would be difficult to be a purist in this matter. Every three years or so the world begins to impress me as grey and pallid, I go have my eyes tested, the ophthalmologist prescribes new glasses, a couple of days later I slide them along the bridge of my nose – and, hey presto, as with a hallucinatory drug, that once grey, pallid world glistens with a new lick of paint. Its colours, which I had merely, passively, been registering, I now *see* again, see as if for the first time in my life. Just as, surely, in our still

from *Becky Sharp*, and whatever may be one's love and nostalgia for black-and-white, one abruptly, actively, sees these elegant young ladies in their red and white and plaid ball gowns, these nonchalant young dragoons whom one half expects to doff their epaulettes to brush a speck of dust from their moustaches. Admit it: even in a book like this, colour makes a difference.

As for Mamoulian himself, he was a curious, contrary sort of director. Like Jean Renoir, about whom I write on the following page, he was an artist who never ceased to innovate: with extreme fluidity of camerawork in *Applause*, with stylized sound effects in *City Streets*, with a subjective point of view in *Dr Jekyll and Mr Hyde*, with integrated musical numbers in *Love Me Tonight* (his sole masterpiece), and so forth. Yet – and here is the contradiction – it's precisely *because of* these innovations that his work strikes us now as so irredeemably dated. It's not that Hollywood was incapable of accommodating innovators (think only of Hitchcock), it's just that Mamoulian appeared more interested in the innovations than in the movies themselves. In *City Streets* he *played* with sound like an infant presented with a toy trumpet. In *Jekyll and Hyde* he *played* with the subjective camera like an infant presented with a gruesome Halloween mask. And in *Becky Sharp* he *played* with colour like an infant presented with a brand new paint box. One might say, whimsically, that his aim was almost always 'off'. He shot sixteen films – and, alas, missed all but one of them.

# 1936 Une partie de campagne

## *A Day in the Country*

Let's be polemical. Jean Renoir, or Renoir *fils,* as some critics affect to call him, has often been proposed as the greatest of all filmmakers. Several of his more eminent colleagues (Welles, for example, who was himself an eligible contender for the title) certainly regarded him as such; and two of his films, *La Règle du jeu* and *La Grande Illusion,* often feature in Top Ten listings. That is an ostensibly unexceptionable judgement which is unlikely to have the reader spluttering with incredulity. But if I were to phrase it differently, if I were to state that Renoir, being the greatest of all filmmakers, is thus not only a greater artist than his father but one of the very greatest artists of our century *in any medium,* the same apparent truism would suddenly acquire an allure of cockeyed improbability and even appear to verge on paradox. Whenever that movable feast of *petits fours,* the cocktail party circuit, plays its favourite game of comparing like with unlike, Joyce with Schoenberg, say, or Picasso with Faulkner, filmmakers still tend to be conspicuously omitted.

It's an omission for which *cinéphiles* themselves, creatures of a fetishistic purism, are in part responsible. When, as will sometimes happen, non-specialized journalists draw up absurd lists of the 'greatest' filmmakers (always the same few accessible household names: Truffaut, Bergman, Fellini, Kurosawa, Woody Allen; never, *never* the supreme geniuses: Griffith, Dreyer, Murnau, Rossellini, Bresson), the film-critical establishment remains oddly uninvolved, as if nothing could be more vulgar than proselytizing, than being a cultural missionary to the uninitiated.

Another cliché. Because of Renoir's halcyon infancy among the Impressionists, his own work is widely assumed to be a filmic extension of that school of painterly sun-dapplers. Yet few of his films surrender to the (more carnal) guise of the Midas curse that afflicted his father, who contrived to turn everything he touched into flesh. One definition of a filmmaker might be *someone who knows where to place his camera,* just as, in the first instance, a painter is someone who knows where to place his brush. Even if a tireless experimenter (with sound in *La Nuit du carrefour,* with documentary realism in *Toni,* with stylized theatricality in *French Cancan* and *Eléna et les Hommes,* with colour in *Le Carrosse d'or* and *The River,* with non-naturalistic acting styles in *Nana* and *Le Testament du Docteur Cordelier,* with televisual shooting techniques in *Le Déjeuner sur l'herbe*), Renoir never lost the secret of exactly where to place his camera: close enough to let the public see what had to be seen yet far enough to respect the dignity and integrity of his actors. There was, to all

of his films, an amazing simplicity, candour, completeness (with every shot, every scene, every situation, the spectator felt he was getting, as with no other filmmaker, *the whole picture*) and, above all, humanity.

And *Une partie de campagne*? A brief (just forty-odd minutes) adaptation of a Maupassant story of a casual and callous courtship conducted during a single day out along the banks of the Loing, it's simultaneously tragic and comic, cruel and elegiac. Nor is there, as you can see, anything stereotypically Renoiresque (as such a qualifier is applied to the influence of Auguste Renoir) in this embrace between Henri (Georges Darnoux) and Henriette (Sylvia Bataille, the then wife of Georges Bataille and future wife of Jacques Lacan). The suggestion, rather, is of the earthier and more corporeal sensuality of a Courbet (horizontal bodies, like felled tree trunks, are *heavy* things). And if, from the shot above, one were to locate what Barthes termed a punctum, that peripheral, unlaboured incidental that nevertheless distracts the spectator's attention from an image's promoted 'meaning', it would surely be the still lighted cigarette in Darnoux's hand, a nearly universal signifier of cavalier Donjuanism and a perfect emblem of Renoir's genius for the telling detail.

As was claimed of the philosopher, nothing human was alien to Jean Renoir. He was an explorer who discovered the world, no less. And it's high time the world, and not merely the world of the cinema, properly discovered him.

# 1937 Make Way for Tomorrow

For reasons that ought to surprise no one, the theme of old age has been shamefully overlooked by the cinema. Yet it has, on occasion, proved capable of prompting both commercial and critical success (Billy Wilder's *Sunset Boulevard* and Robert Aldrich's *Whatever Happened to Baby Jane?*), cult success (Hal Ashby's *Harold and Maude* and Paul Mazursky's *Harry and Tonto*), two of the most original documentary portraits of recent film history (the Maysles brothers' *Grey Gardens* and Hans-Jürgen Syberberg's *Winifred Wagner*) and the melodrama that a happy few of us consider to be the most sublime American movie of the nineteen-seventies, Wilder's *Fedora*. Not to mention the wonderful, terrible *Sextette,* privately financed in 1978, in which an eighty-year-old Mae West – a gorgeous roll of ostrich feathers in her hat recalling nothing so much as Hokusai's Wave, a gloved hand on generous vaudevillian hip, another clutching a tiny, defenceless parasol – resembled one of those monstrous, multi-layered ice-cream confections that are a speciality of the American drugstore.

The most beautiful, tender, funny, heartbreaking of all movies on old age, however, is unquestionably Leo McCarey's *Make Way for Tomorrow*. This is the movie in which Thomas Mitchell (forty-five years old when he made it) and Fay Bainter (also forty-five) play second-generation characters, Victor Moore (sixty-one years old) and Beulah Bondi (forty-five, curiously, but very much older in appearance) the romantic leads. For, unlikely as it sounds, *Make Way for Tomorrow is* an intensely romantic work, enshrining love not at first sight but at last sight, and relating the final days together of an elderly, unwanted couple obliged to separate for ever. Indeed, the film's ending is one of the most astoundingly unhappy in the entire history of the cinema, all the more astounding in that it emerged from a major Hollywood studio. Unable to look after themselves, ruining by their well-intentioned interference the lives of the offspring (Mitchell and Bainter) who have, albeit reluctantly, accepted to lodge them, Moore and Bondi are, as I say, at the close of their marriage, and equally of their lives, their *life,* obliged to separate – one of them to be fobbed off on family in the West, the other headed East. Obliged to separate for ever. Never to see each other again. This, then, is the ending of the inoffensively, sadistically, titled *Make Way for Tomorrow*!

The image opposite is therefore one of those scenes of farewell in railroad stations, scenes familiar from a score of movies, in which two lovers part (for war, usually) and, lost in a forest of waving hands, lyrically enhaloed by poignant billows of steam and smoke, one of them (the woman, usually) forlornly follows the departing train just as far as the station platform will allow her to do – except that, in this instance, I say again, the lovers are sexagenarians,

there is no war and there will be no reunion, ever. I apologize if I seem to be
labouring a point I already made several sentences back, but, like anyone who
sees this extraordinary film, I cannot get over it. And my perplexity is
compounded by the fact that I have no likely means now of ever knowing
whether, in the thirties, there might actually have been a statistical foundation
for such a forced estrangement, whether, in short, as one often muses of
Hollywood's statutory *happy* endings, such a fate ever befell anyone outside of
the cinema.

Just preceding this impossible ending is a magnificent scene in which our
senior-citizen Tristan and Isolde revisit the haunts of their youth and dine for the
very last time in their once favourite restaurant. Watching it, the recollection of a
comparable scene obstinately nagged at me until I realized at last where I had
seen it: in the Big City section of Murnau's *Sunrise*. And, in truth, Victor Moore
and Beulah Bondi might well be the protagonists of that earlier masterpiece,
grown old but not less loving. In a word, *Sunset*.

# 1938 Bringing Up Baby

Howard Hawks has a peculiar status in the American cinema. Ostensibly the most straightforward, most extroverted, of Hollywood filmmakers, he is also, for just that reason, the director whose reputation has most depended on theoretical exegesis. The original auteurists actually referred to themselves as 'Hitchcocko-Hawksians', in homage to the two directors who would eventually dominate their personal Pantheon. But when it came to promoting them to the wider world, Hitchcock was child's play by comparison with Hawks. It is, after all, nearly impossible, when viewing one of Hitchcock's films, not to exclaim, outwardly or inwardly, during one anthology sequence or another, 'What a genius the man is!' With Hawks, on the other hand, and no matter one's admiration (and, indeed, enjoyment) of *Scarface* or *Only Angels Have Wings* or *The Big Sleep* or *Monkey Business* or *Gentlemen Prefer Blondes* or *Rio Bravo*, there is no single locatable element in his apparently bland and beigey-brown universe calculated to elicit any similarly spontaneous effusion. If 'Hawks, or Evidence' was the title of a famous article on the director by Jacques Rivette, that 'evidence', that serene transparency of purpose and design, is paradoxically a quality which requires to be deciphered.

So Hawks himself is still, as ever, an exclusively cultish taste, his sensibility as inaccessible to the larger public of even informed moviegoers as would be that of the most recondite of underground navel-gazers. Yet, as I say, his example was absolutely crucial to the history of auteurism, not because his authorial style screamed at one from the screen but precisely because it didn't. It would no doubt be an exaggeration to claim that no one can appreciate the mystery and beauty of the above movies without having first saturated himself in the entire history of the American cinema, but it's certainly the case that anyone coming to them with an 'innocent' eye is likely to find himself hard-pressed to detect any major difference between them and Hollywood's *vin ordinaire*. It's that which so fascinated the French. Here was a filmmaker who worked within the system, who appeared to respect its most rigid conventions, yet who was meanwhile mining his way, with patience and stealth, to a far more secret, almost indefinable vein of personal inspiration. It is, then, the *latency* of Hawks' achievement (and this applies equally to Nicholas Ray, to Anthony Mann, to Jacques Tourneur, to a host of Hollywood's most *subtly* subversive directors) which has made him such a favourite of true film buffs.

As for *Bringing Up Baby,* it is of course one of Hawks' several screwball comedies. Baby is a leopard, Cary Grant a palaeontologist, Katharine Hepburn a 'madcap' socialite. The daisy-chain structure characteristic of the genre – Grant pursues Baby, Hepburn pursues Grant, Baby pursues Hepburn – clicks into

place from virtually the movie's very first scene. In evidence, too, is the quintessentially Hawksian theme of gender reversal, the comic subversion of virility and its immemorial prerogatives, as that image of ours illustrates.

But the image also reveals a fundamental ambiguity at the core of screwball comedy. As would happen in a number of Cary Grant's movies (notably, Hawks' own *I Was a Male War Bride*), he is seen here without his trousers. And, in fact, it's difficult to think of a pillar of the genre whom one hasn't seen at least once sans pants. If Hawks particularly savoured the spectacle of his leading men, from Grant to Rock Hudson, scampering about in what used to be called their BVDs, there was not a master of screwball humour, Sturges, Capra, Stevens, Wilder, who didn't eventually display his own penchant for pantless heroes. So much so that it sometimes felt as if the only difference between a 'sophisticated' Hollywood comedy and a corny slapstick farce was that in the former the same uncouth knockabout gags as were to be found in the latter would be performed by actors more traditionally associated with debonair nonchalance.

Thus — and it's hard to know whether this is cause for censure (as confirmation of Hollywood's ineradicable crudity) or praise (as an example of its healthy contempt for aesthetic hierarchies) — low comedy was Abbott and Costello being pursued by a leopard, high comedy was Cary Grant and Katharine Hepburn being pursued by a leopard.

89

# 1939  Le Jour se lève

## *Daybreak*

It was Marcel Carné's destiny (a word he himself, indefatigable romancer of fate and its vicissitudes that he was, would not have thought excessive) to witness the unity, cohesion and meaning of his work devastated by the event that its ominously pregnant atmosphere had for so long anticipated – the Second World War. Once, arguably, the most esteemed of all French filmmakers, the standard-bearer of the movement known as 'poetic realism' and the director responsible for having provided published histories of the cinema with a cluster of their most haunting stills (which is not, of course, quite the same thing as making great films), he found himself, after the war, divested of both his talent and his reputation ('disincarnated', as André Bazin pertinently and punningly put it), his own precipitous postwar decline accompanied by a corresponding critical devaluation of his once unassailable pre-war classics.

During the fifties the revisionist young iconoclasts of *Cahiers du Cinéma* (who were later to become the filmmakers of the *nouvelle vague*) argued that these films had been the creations less of Carné himself than of his scenarist, the poet of populist Surrealism, Jacques Prévert; that they were not truly realized *films d'auteur,* the inner visions of an artist transferred directly onto celluloid, but mere illustrations, however brilliant, of another man's scripts; and that the mytho-iconography of poetic realism, with its petty criminals and deserters, its ageing Legionnaires and leather-coated ladies of the night, was essentially a middle-class mystification of Bohemia, synthetic and deliberately depoliticized.

Which is, I suppose, true enough. And yet . . . Perhaps the best way to judge whether such an indictment is fair or not is to ask oneself what precisely it is that one remembers from his films. From *Quai des brumes,* for example, I remember Prévert's dialogue for Jean Gabin and Michèle Morgan – 'Where are you going?' 'I don't know.' 'I'm going your way . . .' – but also Carné's image of Morgan in an ethereally white cellophane raincoat framed against the window of a dockside café. From *Les Portes de la nuit* I remember Carné's meticulous reconstruction of the Paris Métro but also the extreme cynicism of another Prévertian exchange: 'What's happening?' 'Oh, nothing. A woman drowning.' From *Le Jour se lève* I remember the angular street-corner hotel in which a suicidal Gabin is forced to hole up and the exuberantly, unrepentantly corrupt Jules Berry with his troupe of performing dogs. From *Drôle de drame* I remember Louis Jouvet's bemused reiteration of the word 'Bizarre . . .' and from the closing shot of *Les Enfants du paradis,* the director's one undisputed masterpiece, I remember Jean-Louis Barrault's heart-stopping cry of 'Garance!

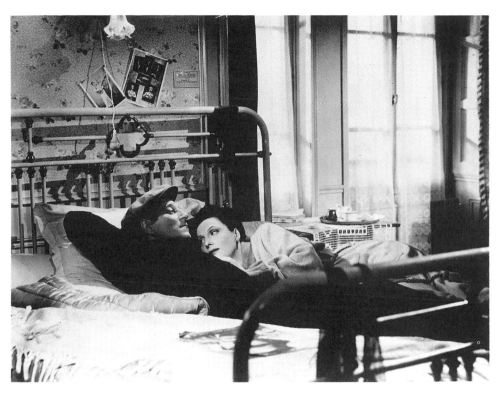

Garance!' as Arletty disappears into a mob of revellers. I remember, too, the soundtrack scores of Joseph Kosma and Maurice Jaubert and the flaccid Gauloises that everyone seemed to smoke and the world-weary faces whose lines could be read like those of a hand and the quite amazing number of Carné's and Prévert's characters who had cause to sigh, at one moment or another, 'C'est drôle, la vie!'

Yes, Carné's films now impinge on our consciousness above all as *memories,* memories often as potent and unshakeable as those of our own lives. And if, as we know, memory plays occasional tricks on us, if the original films, considered strictly as works of art and not as repositories of privileged moments of cinematic myth, were less innovatory than many less familiar works of the same period, it is, after all, the prerogative of memory to be unfairly partial and partisan. In any event, when the mythology of a filmmaker has so seamlessly coincided with the mythology of a nation, it would be absurd to attribute responsibility solely to the contribution of his scenarist.

Of Carné's postwar output, nevertheless, it would be difficult to offer any robust defence, and it now appears almost inconceivable that the man who directed Arletty when she spat out her famous 'Atmosphère . . .! Atmosphère . . .!' on the Canal Saint-Martin bridge in *Hôtel du Nord* could still have been at work a full three decades later while Maoist students were manning barricades along the boulevard Saint-Michel. *C'est drôle, la vie!*

# 1940 Fantasia

In whatever we see on a cinema screen we cannot resist, at some obscure level of our creative imagination, *believing*. Confronted with the sequence in the MGM musical *Anchors Aweigh* in which Gene Kelly performs a droll dance routine with Jerry the cartoon mouse, a New Guinea tribesman (that semi-mythical 'savage' invariably trundled out for every such demonstration) would most likely be incapable of distinguishing between the various layers of reality from which the processed image had been generated – incapable, in short, of grasping that one of the dancers was 'realer' than the other. Yet it's a distinction that even we, sophisticated moviegoers as we flatter ourselves we are, conversant as we have become with the cinema's techniques and technologies, are unable for very long to 'keep in our heads'. Not even we can keep reminding ourselves that Jerry is nothing but an assemblage, a sheaf, of animated drawings. He moves, he dances, he smiles, he grins. He possesses an authentic 'personality'. For the scene's duration at least, he is just as alive for us as Kelly.

Look at the image opposite, from the 'Sorcerer's Apprentice' segment of Walt Disney's *Fantasia,* an image so indelible it has made it practically impossible for most of us to hear the opening bars of the scherzo by Paul Dukas that inspired it, without a subliminal flash of Mickey Mouse calling itself to the attention of our inner eye. What do you see? After the forty-odd photographic stills which preceded it in this book, the forty-odd more or less transparent reflections of living actors and actresses, does Mickey suddenly impress you as any the less *real,* the less vividly *there?* Doesn't it seem as if he too has been arrested in mid-movement – in spite of the fact that the image is but one inanimate drawing from among the thousands which make up the entire sequence? For even as long as it takes to study this still shot, and even given that its 'stillness' dispossesses Mickey of the primary life-simulating property of animation, are you genuinely able to 'keep in your head' the fundamental distance that separates it from all the others I have chosen?

Well, it's upon just this curious psycho-optical effect, this Dalinian persistence of illusion and memory, that the charm and wonderment of the film cartoon is founded – and not just Disney's cartoons, of course, but those of Max Fleischer, Tex Avery, Chuck Jones and Fritz Freleng, the creators of Betty Boop, Droopy, Bugs Bunny, Daffy Duck and the Roadrunner, of the whole celluloid menagerie of the American cinema.

Dali? Dali and Disney? Why not, since the imaginative universes of both of these artists are totalitarian states, in which nary a leaf of grass nor grain of sand can ever quite elude the secret police of their creators' sensibilities. An apple drawn by Disney (or, rather, by one of his team) instantly becomes a Disney

*character*. A Disney cottage could be occupied by no one else but a Disney creation. As they drag their feet behind them in that mastodonic manner peculiar to cartoon characters, Disney's creatures appear to inhabit a world of puff-pastry Surrealism, the strangeness of whose effect is actually intensified by the absence of Surrealist stereotypes. Yet if it's easy enough to envision Goofy consulting one of Dali's soft watches, or Donald Duck's body, after taking a particularly violent pounding, falling open like a Dalinian chest of drawers, the fundamental difference is that, unlike Dali, unquestionably the lesser artist of the two, Disney was a visionary *whose visions were not in the style of visions*.

Ultimately, it matters little whether the cartoons are good or not (and *Fantasia* itself, the Dukas sequence aside, remains unsalvageable kitsch). What matters, instead, is that Disney is what he is, immutably. Both kitsch and culture, both banal and beautiful, his work is situated at the crossroads of extremes.

# 1941 Citizen Kane

A masterpiece, agreed – but nevertheless *not* the greatest film ever made, nor the greatest American film, nor even, so I myself believe, the greatest of Orson Welles' own films. (I have always preferred the sombre sparkle of *The Magnificent Ambersons,* mutilated as it is, and the untrammelled, lunatic licence of *Confidential Report,* his purest and most personal work.) It was far less influential, too, than you might guess from the trumpeting clamour of received wisdom. I chose the accompanying image because it's beautiful and typical of the film and has seldom been reproduced. I chose it, equally, because it illustrates the advent of what seemed to be an entirely new architecture in the American cinema (new, that is, since the silent period), with its great, blank walls, its fireplaces so massive that a touring version of Wagner's *Ring* could be staged inside them without too much strain or squeeze and, most famously, its glowering, cloud-curdled ceilings, ceilings from which the jovially Jovian Welles himself might have hurled a thunderbolt down on his *dramatis personae*. But I chose it, primarily, because it demonstrates the extent to which *Citizen Kane* was to remain *marginal* to film history. For how many subsequent filmmakers were influenced by *that*? Robert Aldrich, possibly, in the fifties (*Kiss Me Deadly, The Big Knife*). Stanley Kubrick in the sixties (*Lolita, Dr Strangelove*). Bernardo Bertolucci in the seventies (*The Spider's Strategy, The Conformist*). Raúl Ruiz, albeit as its parodist, in the eighties. And *Schindler's List* in the nineties (as in the sinister Wellesian swagger with which Liam Neeson's Schindler commandeers the space around him). The postwar cinema took a different route on the whole, its point of departure Rossellini and Italian neo-realism, its culmination the *nouvelle vague* and a seemingly unending succession of national new waves (Latin American, Eastern European, Swiss, Canadian, even British). As Truffaut said, the influence of Welles' film was aspirational rather than professional, in that it prompted more vocations, among future directors and critics, than any other.

What, then, is there still to be said about it? This, perhaps. That it's essentially a backward-looking work, a jigsaw puzzle of film history (just like one of those pored over by Susan Alexander in the pleasure dome of Xanadu, Fla.), where a tracking-shot from Murnau is made to coexist in startling new harmony with an iris dissolve from Griffith. That, even if it was the only one of his works to be released exactly as he intended it, it possesses something of the occult charm that we tend to associate with fragments rather than complete artefacts – Coleridge's *Kubla Khan,* after which Charles Foster Kane was named, is just the most obvious example to come to mind. That, finally, Welles was the sole American filmmaker to have created, as director and actor, a set of characters whose

*names*, as well as faces, we continue to remember. It's even possible to regret (for once) that the cinema is not the theatre and that (short of, unthinkably, remaking Welles' films), it must deny future generations of actors the opportunity of ever reincarnating Kane, Quinlan and Arkadin in revivals of such 'classics'. Roles as exceptional as these are surely potential war-horses in the tradition of Marguerite Gautier and Cyrano de Bergerac.

Jean Giraudoux once wrote: 'Il n'y a pas d'oeuvres, il n'y a que des auteurs' ('There are no works of art, there are only creators'), and although he was employing the term 'auteur' in its conventional, pre-cinéphilic connotation, it certainly can be applied to Orson Welles. He was the life and soul of the cinema, as of a party. He was the medium's only actor-manager of the old, flea-bitten Henry Irvingish school, overacting in other people's bad movies, overdirecting his own masterpieces and, as it were, overliving his own life. His curse, yet it was arguably also his salvation, wasn't merely to have been interrupted, like Coleridge, by a person from Porlock. It was, wilfully, perversely, to have chosen Porlock – in a word, Hollywood – as the place in which to build his Xanadu.

# 1942  Sullivan's Travels

Unmistakably, a screwball comedy by Preston Sturges – indeed, *the* screwball comedy by Preston Sturges. *Sullivan's Travels* is not necessarily Sturges' finest film (my own choice would be *The Palm Beach Story,* made in the same year) but, functioning as both a defence and an apotheosis of the whole genre, it's undoubtedly his most important. In it Joel McCrea plays Sullivan, a successful Hollywood director of undemanding comedies, *Ants in Your Pants of 1941* being the most recent. The forties are troubled times, however, and Sullivan acquires first a conscience then, in an uncontrollable itch to *edify,* the rights to a best-selling, high-minded novel, *Brother, Where Art Thou?* While researching the novel's theme, he is entangled in a knot of misadventures that would defy any easy encapsulation and eventually finds himself the prisoner of a chain gang. At which point, watching how a knockabout Mickey Mouse cartoon has enabled his fellow convicts to forget, however fleetingly, the wretchedness of their condition, he comes to understand where his (and Hollywood's?) noblest vocation lies.

Curiously, though, Joel McCrea doesn't figure in this still. Its quartet of males belongs rather to the film's supporting cast, often the true glory of Sturges' cinema and of the screwball comedy in general. Who are they? I know their faces, to be sure, I've seen them in a hundred movies ('Oh, it's *him*!'), but the names, the names . . . In this particular shot I find I can identify the dapper, moustachioed gent on the far right (Franklin Pangborn), the stocky fellow seated at his feet (William Demarest) and, if now a little more shakily, the man standing behind the desk with a cigar in his mouth (Porter Hall?). But the fourth? I could look him up, certainly, and maybe, for my credibility as a critic, I ought to – except that I've seen him, too, in scores of films and have never felt the need to know precisely who he might be.

For some of us these performers, nameless or not, were the real stars. For some of us the Hollywood star-system was also a system of supporting players. For some of us, I repeat, anyone arguing that the American cinema hasn't suffered a decline in recent years must be blind to the way in which the middle distance of movies from the thirties, forties and fifties (comedies in particular) was routinely enhanced by this unmatched repertory company. And what was most significant about these teeming secondary figures was the ease with which vividness of typology was achieved without recourse to the (novelist's or dramatist's) primary mnemonic strategy of according their characters names.

During its thirty-year heyday (roughly from 1925 to 1955) Hollywood approached more closely than any of its rival art forms the paradigmatic perfection of the *commedia dell'arte.* In the *commedia dell'arte* (which means

'the comic drama of the professional players', a perfect definition of the typical
American movie) each character was instantly identified by his name: thus
Arlecchino, the droll, nimble-witted servant; Pantalone, the Venetian magnifico;
Dottore Gratiano, the gullible, lecherous advocate; and so forth. In the
American cinema the typology was no less unfailingly graphic and
instantaneous, except that it was not on the characters' but the *actors*' names
(and often, as I say, only their faces) that it was founded. If one saw Edward
Everett Horton's name on a film's credits, one just *knew* he would portray a
dithering milquetoast; Eric Blore, a sarcastic, tight-lipped manservant;
Margaret Hamilton, a sour, hatchet-profiled schoolmarm; Eugene Pallette, a
kindly, spluttering paterfamilias; Una Merkel, a wisecracking, saucer-eyed
stenographer; Ralph Bellamy, an ingenuous, kindly and invariably frustrated
suitor.

   As anyone addicted to the constant replenishment of old movies on television
is aware, these performers and scores like them were what distinguished the
Hollywood product from that of every competing national cinema. And it's
because *they* have disappeared, never to be replaced, that, as Norma Desmond
protests in *Sunset Boulevard* when it's suggested that she used to be 'big', 'It's
the pictures that got small.'

# 1943 I Walked With a Zombie

You *cannot* be serious! How, they might ask, for whom the name of Jacques Tourneur and the title of his film are equally closed books, how can something called *I Walked With a Zombie* merit inclusion in an album enshrining the most mysterious and enduring images of the cinema's first (and maybe only) century? As for those, by contrast, who *are* conversant with both filmmaker and film, who are aware, precisely, of their respective merits and who thus take exception to the notion that special pleading is required to justify their inclusion, I would merely suggest that they attempt to decrust that terrible title of the neutralizing patina of film-buff familiarity and remind themselves just how it must sound to the non-initiate chancing across it for the first time. This book is designed for those both outside and inside the charmed circle; and unless the former are prepared to acknowledge that a film called *I Walked With a Zombie* might be worth discussing, and the latter that it nevertheless continues to pose a cultural problem, it won't really work as it should.

Its title notwithstanding, Tourneur's *I Walked With a Zombie* is a vision of horror worthy of Poe, of Lovecraft, of Géricault, that lifelong imaginer of nightmares (dreams) and night mares (horses), a complex cobweb spun out of light and shadow, of black and white, in the purest tradition of Hollywood chiaroscuro. And why not zombies, when all is said and done? Speculating on why Sir Arthur Bliss's ballet of the nineteen-fifties, *The Lady of Shalott,* has never been revived, the critic Jann Parry mooted that 'perhaps the time is past for spellbound ladies, medieval knights and mysterious deaths'. She is doubtless right. Yet a contemporary counterpart of the atmospherically romantic iconography that has always been classical ballet's stock-in-trade might well be what is generally regarded as not just the last, fetid gasp of the Romantic Agony but also, handily, the defining genre of the contemporary cinema of exploitation, *horror. Les Sylphides,* after all, the original Romantic ballet, with its sylphs and wraiths, its sprites and fairies, might easily have been retitled, with only a modicum of narrative revision, *I Danced With a Zombie.*

I ordinarily don't care for horror films, bad or good. If bad, I simply can't see the point; if good (Murnau's *Nosferatu,* Dreyer's *Vampyr,* James Whale's two *Frankenstein* films at Universal in the thirties, a couple of Roger Corman's Poe adaptations with Vincent Price), I am genuinely haunted by them. I have never forgotten the rats in *Nosferatu,* the flour-mill in *Vampyr* or the final shot of one of Corman's films, when the camera, remaining behind inside a locked torture chamber which, we are told, will never be opened again, slowly tracks towards that instrument of Inquisitorial torment named the Iron Maiden, closer and closer, until we are able to see a pair of doomed and demented eyes staring out at

us from between its bars — and I fancy I will go to my death with these images and their implications still vividly intact in my head. Who, as they say, needs it?

But the movies made by Tourneur for the producer Val Lewton (which also include *Cat People* and *The Leopard Man*) are above all (in the sense intended by Cocteau when he defined the cinema as a dream which the whole audience dreams together) shared nightmares, nightmares capable of, paradoxically, *awakening* our unconscious fears and fantasies, nightmares, too, it has to be said, tending to reinforce our profoundest prejudices — of misogyny on occasion, of racism frequently. For take a look, in the image above, at the white woman who has 'fallen awake', so to speak, in the shade of the black man. Take a look at this symbol of the elemental fragility of white in pitch darkness — the darkness of a race as much as of a room. Look, now, at the black man himself, a man conspicuously the colour of his own shadow. Look at his squat nose, his pug Negroid lips, his prominent Adam's apple. It's not, I would say, by chance that he is shown standing in profile — for this is the black man of white supremacist myth, the black man just down from the banana trees, the black man as if only just risen off his forelegs to pose for a white man's chart on the evolution of mankind.

# 1944  Nuit et Brouillard
## *Night and Fog*

No, it isn't what you first thought it was when you turned the page. These are shoes, only shoes, thousands of pairs of shoes. The corpses, if you will, of thousands of pairs of shoes, but nothing but shoes nevertheless. Shoes that were once worn by thousands of people – people of whom it may be said that one would not have wished to be in their shoes.

It's a still from Alain Resnais' short documentary film *Night and Fog,* which, although it was actually made in 1956, used footage that had been shot, often by the Nazis themselves, by the very personnel of the concentration camps, in the early nineteen-forties. And if it's impossible not to interpret this still as a visual metaphor for the mounds of corpses by which these shoes were once worn, it need be done so only in the most general terms imaginable. The photograph is horrible not simply because of the reality that lies directly behind it. It's horrible *because it's the photograph of a mound,* and, in the second, post-Holocaust, half of this century, every photograph of a mound – a mound of practically anything – is horrible by definition.

If the aura of the Sacred may be said to have enhaloed the twentieth century, the 'terrible century' in Hannah Arendt's phrase, it's in relation to the Holocaust. *Night and Fog* was released, as I have said, in 1956, just twelve years after the liberation and revelation of the camps. Since when, attempts have regularly been made by the cinema to address the theme, most of them from Europe (Andrzej Munk's *Passenger,* Gillo Pontecorvo's *Kapo*), a mere handful from Hollywood (Stanley Kramer's *Judgment at Nuremberg,* the television mini-series *Holocaust*). Yet only Claude Lanzmann's *Shoah,* which eschewed Holocaust imagery altogether, deserves to be placed alongside Resnais' film. And *Schindler's List*? When I asked a young acquaintance of mine, who had finally caught up with *Night and Fog* on video, about his impression of it, he replied, 'It reminds me of Spielberg's film, except that it isn't as well made.'

A few shameless miscalculations aside (notably, Schindler's last leave-taking from 'his' Jews, as maudlin and unnecessarily protracted as the endless ending of *E. T.*), *Schindler's List* was not at all the disgrace one had every right to expect. It was still, however, a monstrosity. It was, after all, a Hollywood film like any other Hollywood film (the first words one saw on the screen were 'Amblin Entertainment') and it was shot like any other Hollywood film. It had an unusually lengthy shoot in Europe (although not at Auschwitz itself, as Spielberg had hoped) and a cast, probably, of thousands. And what I see when I watch the film, what, hard as I try, I cannot prevent myself from seeing, is that cast being

put through its paces on some foggy, nocturnal location, put through its paces
by the boyishly handsome director himself in his snazzy windcheater, his red
N. Y. Yankees baseball cap, his granny glasses and his beard. I see him blowing
into his cupped hands and pointing a gloved index finger as directors do. I see
the bony, skeletal extras, in striped pyjamas or else stark naked, laughing and
joking and jostling one another (why not? It's their right) while waiting for a
new shot to be set up. I see the make-up artists applying a few final touches to
the corpses which these extras will have to disinter with their bony, skeletal bare
hands. I see the first take that doesn't quite 'take' and the bony, skeletal extras
relaxing, shaking the pins and needles out of their bony, skeletal limbs, smoking
cigarettes, having surreptitious pees, complaining about the night and the fog
(why not? It's their right). And I think, dear Steven Spielberg: What a comment
on the filmmaker's vocation. Brilliant as your film undoubtedly is, what a
disgusting way to make a living.

# 1945 Detour

What, in popular mythology, is the codified image of the American film industry? It is, supremely, an image of Hollywood, Hollywood as a palmy square mile of seven studios, Metro-Goldwyn-Mayer, Warner Brothers, 20th Century-Fox, Paramount, Columbia, RKO and Universal, neighbouring one another like the colleges of an ancient English university. These studios, too (again as popularly conceived), were laid out in so many campuses, whose residents, disguised, as though for an arts ball, as cowboys or Cossacks or Assyrian slaves, would stroll along its leafy pathways with scripts, rather than copies of *Beowulf,* under their arms. And, of course, each studio had its specific house style: so much so that, if some practical joker of a projectionist were to have tacked MGM's title card onto a velvety, nocturnal Fox thriller with Dana Andrews and Linda Darnell, the experience, for an unsuspecting movie buff, would be as unsettling as tasting coffee after ordering tea. (Such niceties, alas, are a thing of the past. One can no longer see an American film 'blind' and instantly know from which studio it emerged, the vineyard and the vintage.)

What is forgotten in this already roseate evocation is that there were also studios located on the other side of the tracks, on so-called Poverty Row, studios like Republic (which, among countless thick-ear westerns and thrillers, nevertheless produced Nicholas Ray's *Johnny Guitar* and John Ford's *The Quiet Man*) and Monogram (to which Jean-Luc Godard dedicated *A bout de souffle*) and PRC, or Producers Releasing Corporation. It was PRC, a company, as one commentator observed, 'notorious for its ineptitude', that was responsible for Edgar G. Ulmer's *Detour.* It was PRC that forced Ulmer to shoot the movie in six days with absolutely nothing in the way of production values. It was PRC that saddled him with, as his 'stars', Tom Neal and Ann Savage, two names scarcely calculated to ring down the ages. And it was PRC that released the publicity still above, which is indeed of such disarming ineptitude that, apart from the total omission of any compositional ingredient likely to persuade a potential exhibitor to screen it or a potential paying customer to purchase a ticket, its photographer didn't even know enough to request the gentleman (a technician? an extra? Ulmer himself?) half but only half-concealed in the door jamb to stand aside for the photograph to be taken. If there exists such a thing as a first draft of a shot, as of a sentence, this surely is it.

Somehow, though, *Detour,* about a hitchhiker (Neal – and how, one wonders, watching such a born loser, did he ever survive *into* the film in the first place?) who freakishly entangles himself with one of the most hellish heroines in the history of the cinema, is a masterpiece, the very finest (*ex aequo* with Joseph E. Lewis' *Gun Crazy*) of all B-movies. Nor is it a masterpiece despite but, like all

the great B-movies, because of its unpromising origins. Because of the virtual
absence of sets, exteriors in particular, Ulmer was obliged to improvise, using
lighting alone (and lots of dry ice) to create an atmosphere. Because of the
ludicrous shooting schedule that had been imposed on him, he achieved an
economy of narrative and liberty of expression comparable to that which we
would attribute, twenty years later, to the *nouvelle vague*. Because of his miserly
budget, he contrived to invest the film's visual style with what might be called
the poetry of the threadbare, that same 'cheap' poetry that an utterly redundant
movie like Warren Beatty's *Dick Tracy* would spend upward of forty million
dollars to recreate. And so it happened that the *material* constraints of Poverty
Row became, for a director as inventive as Ulmer, a set of productive *aesthetic*
constraints, not so very different, in a sense, from the Aristotelian unities.

There exist branches of modern mathematics in which $-10$, let's say, is rated
as a higher number than $+5$ on the grounds that it's *farther from zero*. It's easy,
on occasion, to smile at Ulmer's films, and B-movies in general, for their
technical inadequacies; yet they have often proved more enduring than the
so-called A-movies that they were designed to accompany and support. Let me,
then, salute in Edgar G. Ulmer an artist who, refusing to be engulfed by the
yawning open mouth of zero, once and for all time pitched his tent far from the
shores of mediocrity.

# 1946 It's a Wonderful Life

A spangly Christmas tree, a garlanded living room, a gathering of friends, relatives and children, smiling yet also solicitous, as though having only just emerged from an ordeal – a tableau, in short, a tableau in the purest Norman Rockwell style (look, merely, at the little boy cupping his cheeks in the centre foreground). It's the end, the patently happy end, of a film, but by what circuitous route did the film reach this shot?

Everyone has seen Frank Capra's *It's a Wonderful Life*. Hence everyone must know that, in it, James Stewart plays a small-town businessman driven to the very brink of suicide by a combination of personal inadequacy (as he believes) and professional insolvency. At the eleventh hour, however, this being a Capra movie, his guardian angel descends to earth to accord him a vision of Bedford Falls, the town in which he has lived his entire life, as it would have become had he never been born. The cosy little burg is transformed, during an extraordinary fantasy sequence, into a stylized hellhole of squalid rooming houses and garish honky-tonk bars, virtually all of them the property of one man, a scheming, curmudgeonly Scrooge (Lionel Barrymore, needless to say) whose chronic rascality is at the origin of Stewart's financial ruin.

But which, ultimately, is the illusion and which the reality? Would it be a trifle glib to suggest that it isn't the fantasy sequence but *the rest of the movie* which constitutes the true dream of *It's a Wonderful Life*; that the Utopian Americana, the *Saturday Evening Post* Utopiana, exemplified by its closing tableau, is infinitely more of a fantasy than those rooming houses and bars which do indeed (now, if not in 1946) dot the industrial hinterland of the United States? The genius of Capra, as of an enduring strain of sentimental populism in the American cinema (one might cite the Andy Hardy cycle, *Meet Me in St. Louis*, *Miracle on 34th Street*, *E. T.*), was to have reinvented a quintessentially nineteenth-century dream of Christmas (*It's a Wonderful Life* is very precisely the filmic equivalent of *A Christmas Carol*) in the context of the quintessential art form of the twentieth century, reinvented it with such a preternatural force and vision (which was, in Capra's case, an immigrant's vision) as to persuade more than one spectator, for ninety minutes or so, that the terms *Christmas* and *America* might be synonymous.

Which is to say, Christmas and America as the twin mythic repositories of a set of values (family, marriage, monogamy) that had long since been abandoned by every art form but the cinema. For consider: when Stewart, horrified by his descent into a hypothetical hell, asks his guardian what has, or would have, happened to the childhood sweetheart whom he had married (and who is played by Donna Reed), the elderly, pixilated celestial at first displays a strange

reluctance to respond; until, threatened with physical abuse from his now half-demented ward, he blurts out in a strangulated voice, 'She's just about to close up the library!'

*She's just about to close up the library*. Which means, to all intents and purposes: she is an old maid. In Hollywood's symbology the library has always been an unmistakable signifier of failure, of solitude and (if the librarian happens to be a woman) of prim, mousy, bespectacled, hair-in-a-bun plainness, a fact which Capra, one of the cinema's great naïve communicators, knew his audience would instinctively understand. Yet he was even cannier, far cannier, than that, manipulating such a convention not only as a shortcut to understanding but the better to communicate his absolute faith in the dominant values of his adopted country. Think, after all, of what the revelation of Reed's spinsterhood actually means, of the unparalleled idealization of romantic love and fidelity which it implies: that marriage to another man would have been unimaginable for her *even if Stewart had never existed.*

# 1947 Black Narcissus

'Of course all films are surrealist. They are because they are making something that looks like a real world but isn't.'

Thus spoke Michael Powell, one of the very few British directors to have been granted a year to himself in this book, and one whose fame and reputation have done nothing but flourish since his death. In recent years, indeed, Powell has so often been written about as a neglected artist (as often by his fellow directors, Martin Scorsese and Bertrand Tavernier, for example, as by critics or historians) that he is fast turning into one of the most exhaustively documented of all filmmakers. Yet, in the context of the British cinema's apparently incorrigible penchant for genteel 'realism', he remains a genuine test case, which is why it would have been unthinkable to omit him from a celebration of film history. The best study of his, and his partner Emeric Pressburger's, work is still Ian Christie's *Arrows of Desire*; and what makes that such an inspired choice of title, apart from its obvious reference to the bull's-eye trademark of their production company, The Archers, is that the verse which in Blake's 'Jerusalem' rhymes with 'Bring me my arrows of desire' is 'Bring me my chariot of fire', Christie thereby offering a neat encapsulation of two diametrically opposed visions of the British cinema.

The Archers were authentic originals, yes, but were their arrows truly tipped with the life-giving poison of desire? That the still opposite, from *Black Narcissus*, seems scarcely to belong to the British cinema at all, agreed. That the abused word 'surrealist' is for once the appropriate one, there can be no question. That, from a pallid Rumer Godden novel about a squad of hysterical nuns cloistered in the Himalayas, Powell and Pressburger produced an extraordinarily potent concoction of rampant exoticism, stylized settings (the movie was shot entirely in the studio) and exquisite colours (Powell was the British cinema's sole, if more than occasionally garish, colourist), to be sure. Yet, all that said, what is left is the film itself, not its subject matter, not its reputation, not even its infallibly gorgeous imagery. And one discovers, rather to one's disappointment, that the object of its fabled sexiness turns out to be David Farrar's knees, of all unlikely, unlovely things: as the local Maharajah's agent, Farrar suggestively lolls around the virginal dovecote in khaki shorts. For artists famed for their kinky imagination, Powell and Pressburger rarely succeeded in shaking off a very British sense of the proprieties.

Where they did excel was in belying Truffaut's notorious claim of a fundamental incompatibility between Britain, as visual raw material, and the cinema. Half-Tories, half-dreamers, they could hardly have been better equipped for the task. By transforming cartoonist David Low's pompous, blinkered archetype into a choleric if adorable old codger, they made *The Life and Death of Colonel Blimp* not just an elegy for the English military caste that Low

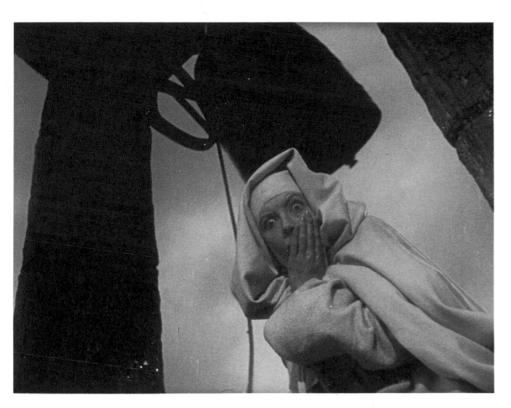

abominated but a film with something of the magical whimsicality of a Stanley Spencer fresco. Commissioned in 1946 to devise a propaganda film that might contribute to easing the then strained Anglo-American alliance, they came up with *A Matter of Life and Death*, a droll crypto-Chestertonian fantasy about an aviator plummeting headlong from his blazing aircraft and, although already officially booked into the hereafter, somehow surviving. And Powell alone, at the end of his career, when his work was becoming frankly artsy-fartsy, still contrived to make what was his most personal film, *Peeping Tom*, an outlandishly creepy masterpiece whose violence and sexual candour revolted the critics of the period but which has since been rehabilitated as a masterly exploration of filmic voyeurism, a conclusive demonstration of the implicitly pornographic nature of the medium.

Yet I cannot help thinking of the director of whom I am just about to write, Hitchcock. As a filmmaker, Hitchcock was *himself* a Peeping Tom, a voyeur, and he inveigled the spectator into becoming one as well. Hitchcock lived out his obsessions *through* celluloid whereas Powell could only record his *on* celluloid. In each of his films Hitchcock not only made his celebrated cameo appearances, he unashamedly (even if perhaps unconsciously) exposed himself in every frame, almost as if his psyche were being strip-searched, whereas Powell's innate sense of decorum couldn't help acting as a permanent curb on his bravura assaults upon the canons of good taste. And, of course, Hitchcock went to America while Powell stayed in Britain – and Britain, unfortunately, stayed in Powell.

# 1948  Rope

And so there was Hitch. Alfred Hitchcock was a chess master who played blindfold against himself; a poet, like Chesterton, who attempted to decode messages which he himself had sent; a detective, like Chesterton's Father Brown, who attempted to solve puzzles which he himself had set; a genius, like Chesterton's Man Who Was Sunday, who slowly and insidiously expanded until he seemed almost to coincide with the cinema in its totality; a cultivator of the purple patch, or set-piece, which is what we really mean when we describe him as the 'Master of Suspense'; a director for whom the cinema was one of the fine arts, as murder was for De Quincey, and for whom a studio sound stage was a kind of operating theatre ('Lights! Action! Cut!') in which to carry out his nightmarish experiments; a criminal who committed his crimes by exclusively cinematic means (in the shower-murder sequence of *Psycho* the real mutilation of Janet Leigh was performed, as we know, not on the set itself but during what must have been terrifying sessions at the editing table); a gambler who possessed a virtually infallible system (whereas most directors bet everything they have on a single lucky number); an Englishman who made some of the finest British films ever – such entertainments of enduring bewitchment as *The Lodger, Blackmail, The Man Who Knew Too Much, The Thirty-Nine Steps, The Lady Vanishes* and *Young and Innocent* (remarkable for its amazing overhead shot tracking the entire length of a ballroom of dancers before zeroing in on the twitching black-faced minstrel murderer like a Scud missile) – he made all these marvellous films then simply upped and left for Hollywood, where he would make a succession of even finer ones (*Shadow of a Doubt, Notorious, Strangers on a Train, Rear Window, Vertigo, North by Northwest, The Birds, Marnie*); and, finally, for the young French critics and directors-to-be who would be instrumental in reinventing his reputation for the greater good of cinema history, notably Truffaut, Rohmer, Chabrol and Godard, he was exactly what Edgar Allan Poe had been for his French poet-translators, Baudelaire, Mallarmé and Valéry, a century before: a visionary artist of so rich and strange an imaginative universe that it had a cathartic impact on an artistic tradition that, to all outward appearances, could scarcely have been more distant from it.

That is a very long sentence, appropriately so for a film like *Rope,* whose narrative unfolds in just ten shots, ten single-take sequences lasting precisely ten minutes each (a film camera cannot shoot longer than ten minutes at one time without being reloaded). And, given the challenge posed by these sequence-shots – during which whole complex scenes unreel without a single cut, scenes which therefore require not just that the film's spatial parameters be meticulously plotted out in advance (how the camera will move, how the performers will

move in, out and across the screen) but also that the shoot itself run its course without a hitch, so to speak, without any actor fluffing his lines or blocking another's space – it's worth reminding ourselves that what actually makes a long take so seductive is not what is natural but what is artificial about it. The eye edits and the camera blinks. 'Cutting', in one sense or another, is natural to both, and the human eye tends to find a film which has been edited far easier to interpret, to *read,* than one which has not. Which is why *Rope* is such a quintessentially Hitchcockian thriller. For, in addition to the suspense implicit in its plot (a pair of Nietzschean dandies murder a close personal friend merely to demonstrate their own intellectual superiority), it generates an even more powerful *meta-suspense* through the very technique by which Hitchcock has opted to film it. *How long is this shot going to last*? we nail-bitingly ask ourselves. *Surely a cut is due any second now*? And (even if common sense tells us that nothing of the kind can possibly occur in a completed film) *is one of the performers about to make a wrong move*? The paradox of a shot as emblematically cinematic as the ten-minute take is that what it ultimately mimics are the tensions of the real, of the *live* experience.

In the image opposite, clearly, the film is not yet under way. The room in which it is set is empty. But Hitchcock himself is present, already there, eerily so.

# 1949 Stromboli

Once each decade the journal *Sight and Sound* polls a hundred-odd critics on their selection of the ten greatest films of cinema history. A little tiresomely, this poll of polls has for the last four decades elected *Citizen Kane* the best of all, and there seems no good reason not to anticipate that it will go on doing so. Of rather more interest than the results, however, is the manner in which individual listings reveal the tastes of succeeding generations of *cinéphiles*. Those, for example, whose involvement with the medium dates from its pre-auteurist period still tend to plump for the (to a contemporary eye) smugly humanistic works that would appear to have marked them for life: Vsevolod Pudovkin's *Mother*, Milestone's *All Quiet on the Western Front*, Vittorio De Sica's *Umberto D,* and so on. From the auteurist critics of the early sixties, by contrast, there's a noticeable bias towards more juicily accessible items like *Rio Bravo, North by Northwest* and Max Ophüls's *Madame de . . .* (For the most extreme auteurists, in fact, the choice tends to be phonetically polarized: *Madame de . . .* vs *Umberto D.*) And from the overtly politicized critics of the seventies comes a whole other set of titles.

But one once prominent title which is fast disappearing from all such lists is Roberto Rossellini's *Stromboli*. Indeed, the prefix to the school to which it belongs, neo-realism, may eventually have to be replaced by 'retro', as no cinematic movement is at present less in vogue. The American auteurist critic Andrew Sarris scoffed at neo-realist movies as 'male weepies'; for Cocteau, on the other hand, they were modernized Arabian Night tales in which the camera would roam the streets disguised as a beggar. Whoever was right, the question does not truly concern *Stromboli,* a film which far transcends any narrowly defined neo-realist ethos.

We all know the principles of that ethos: the shooting on actual locations; the use of non-professional actors (in *La Prise de pouvoir par Louis XIV,* a French film made as late as 1966, Rossellini went so far as to cast an unknown in the role of a king); the strong focus on the (by the cinema) often neglected social strata of the working-class poor and unemployed. Rossellini mostly respected these principles, albeit exploiting them to entirely different ends from those which interested a sentimental old neo-realist softie like De Sica. Particularly in his collaborations with Ingrid Bergman, which also included *Europa '51, Viaggio in Italia* and *Die Angst,* he was the supreme *documentist (sic:* these films were documents not documentaries) of the European postwar malaise and arguably the most important filmmaker working anywhere in the world between 1945 and 1955.

*Stromboli* is the account of a stateless Lithuanian, Karin (Bergman), who

succeeds in escaping the grim austerities of a camp for displaced persons by marrying an uncouth fisherman from the island of the film's title, a barren, friendless trap that she has fantasized as an archetypal Hollywood 'isle', idyllic and practically palm-fringed. And, watching it, one has the impression that if Rossellini had opted to focus on the individual, *any individual,* next to Karin in the camp, his or her story would no less hauntingly have characterized the post-apocalypse *zeitgeist*. But then, almost all of his work from these years is marked by just such a terrifying demographic *randomness,* a randomness that, for the Catholic Rossellini, could only be exorcized, as it is in the case of Karen herself (who must confront alone the mindless and earthily 'Mediterranean' violence of an erupting volcano), by the ultimate annihilation of all narrative: the revelation of God.

It matters little, then, that, as radiantly chic in her sweater and slacks as if she had just popped in from a photographic session, Bergman makes for a faintly improbable DP. It was the principle of neo-realism, after all, that in the cinema just as in life everyone is, from the most Godlike of overviews, only a supporting performer. And it made no difference to Rossellini, as it would not to God Himself, that that supporting performer was a star.

# 1950 Los Olvidados
## *The Young and the Damned*

To what is one immediately sensitive in this grotesque tableau from Luis Buñuel's *Los Olvidados?* Of, I would propose, an extraordinary intensification of the *physical*. No matter how ambiguous their status (are they young men? children? midgets?), the three figures whom it presents to us are, in the sense of the Jamesian nuance, tremendously *there*. There is, in this image, what might be called an unselective accentuation of detail, a paradoxically uniform emphasis overall. Thus one's eye is drawn almost as much to the abnormally ballooning crotches of the two figures on the left as to the features of their ageless faces. Thus, too, one is as uneasily conscious of the oddly telescoped torso of the figure on the extreme left as of the apparent absence of any neck on the shoulders of the strange little fellow in the middle. And what one notices above all, no doubt, is the saw-toothed corrugation of the hat brim on the left and its more muted mirroring by that on the right. That corrugation, indeed, like the disquietingly luminous glass of milk which, in Hitchcock's *Suspicion*, Cary Grant bears upstairs to Joan Fontaine or the Louise Brooks wig which Anna Karina wears in Godard's *Vivre sa vie*, constitutes one of those ostensibly peripheral details with which one finds oneself just as fascinated as with any of the film's characters and which may remain lodged in one's memory longer than most of the codified parameters (plot, character psychology, camera movements) by which the medium is supposed to communicate its fund of meanings.

The image is in fact of a trio of children, urchins from the slums of Mexico City, but they could hardly be more different from those, redeemed *in extremis* by their dishevelled cuteness, of De Sica's *Sciuscia* or Mira Nair's *Salaam Bombay!* Beyond everything else that has been said about Buñuel, beyond his surrealistico-marxistico-freudian abomination of social inequalities (in *Las Hurdes, Viridiana, Nazarin, Tristana*), beyond his exploration of the very frontiers of rationality (in *Un chien andalou, L'Age d'or, Le Fantôme de la liberté*), beyond his teasing anticlericalism (in *Simón del Desierto, La Voie lactée*) and deadpan parody of upper-crust mores (*Le Journal d'une femme de chambre, Belle de Jour, Le Charme discret de la bourgeoisie*), the distinguishing element of his work is surely the indelible *thereness* of his performers, be it the tramps of *Viridiana* or the one-legged Catherine Deneuve of *Tristana*, be it the tall, Beardsleyan Pierre Clémenti in *Belle de Jour*, his mouth a mesmeric mess of corkscrewily asymmetrical gold teeth, or Clémenti's near-double, the androgynous, dandified protagonist of *Un chien andalou* who, chancing on a severed hand in the street, neurotically worries at it with his cane.

Buñuel is a very great director, of that there has never been any question – his oeuvre is one of the least contested in cinema history. Yet, just as he initiated that oeuvre with a deliberately *unwatchable* image (a razor slicing a human eye in *Un chien andalou,* an eye that looks, to those who are able to keep their own eyes open during the sequence, like a statue's gobbet of spit), so its true significance only emerges in relation to everything in the medium to which it offers a resounding slap in the face. Those filmmakers, past and present, who have treated the cinema as one of the decorative arts, on a par with hairdressing and interior decorating. Those directors, not necessarily untalented, who are content to remain good studio hirelings, not precisely yes-men but 'yes, but . . .' men. Those so-called artists whose misty-lensed brand of pictorialism amounts to little more than screen-dressing (as one says 'window-dressing'). And that legion of critically esteemed films that are 'stylish' rather than made in any specific style, such stylishness representing, in film-world parlance, a question less of formal or thematic innovation than of immaculate taste and what used to be described as 'class'.

Buñuel never gave a shit for taste or class, the cult of glamour or the apotheosis of gloss. Which is possibly why his films have *always* been admired and were never obliged to traverse that posthumous purgatory to which even the finest of filmmakers have fallen victim. But then, of course, the old atheist never did believe in purgatory.

# 1951 Rio Grande

O chestnut tree, great rooted blossomer,
Are you the leaf, the blossom or the bole?
O body swayed to music, O brightening glance,
How can we know the dancer from the dance?

W. B. Yeats, of course, from 'Among School Children'. Study, now, from John Ford's *Rio Grande,* this prototypically Fordian shot of a flag-bearing line of cavalrymen, with John Wayne at its helm. Is this an image of narrative (these cavalry soldiers are presumably bound somewhere, on a mission of import to the movie's plot)? Or is it an image of style (no matter where they might be bound, the shot itself is unmistakeably from a Ford western, from *Rio Grande,* as I say, but it might equally have been from *Fort Apache* or, if in colour, from *She Wore a Yellow Ribbon* or *The Horse Soldiers* or *Two Rode Together,* in which other, similarly Remingtonian cavalrymen would have been riding out on other missions of other import to other narratives)? How, in short, can we know the dancer from the dance?

A genre is a program, in the sense of the word as it's employed of computer software. And even if the western initially impresses one as an inherently closed, ungiving genre, it too has permitted various filmmakers to reinvent it at will. While those of Anthony Mann and Budd Boetticher, with their majestic natural locations, their vast lowering clouds (hung so low in the heavens you feel the movie's characters will have to crawl under them) and their great sudden thunderstorms (as if God had just blown into a cosmic paper bag and burst it over the world), tend to conform to the basic popular conception of the genre, others no less central to the canon manage to annex many of the codes and practices of genres that might have seemed totally antithetical to them. Fred Zinnemann's *High Noon,* for example, is as much an urban thriller as it is a western proper, Nicholas Ray's *Johnny Guitar* is a melodrama, Raoul Walsh's *Pursued* a film noir, George Marshall's *Destry Rides Again* a screwball comedy.

As for Ford's westerns, the form itself, as the quote from Yeats was intended to suggest, is subsumed within the expression of the director's own individualism, his personal iconography, to a degree unusual for so convention-bound a genre. Several of them, too, are not westerns at all but movies about the family — and, particularly, about the extended male family of the army. In this sense, if Ford may be compared with any artist, it's not with one of his fellow filmmakers but with a novelist, Kipling. With Kipling's apologiae of the Raj, after all, his westerns share the equivocal endorsement of colonial adventurism, the omnipresent undertow of racial tension, the unexpectedly subtle psychology,

the truculent non-coms (Victor McLaglan, one of Ford's regular repertory company of supporting actors, could have stepped straight from the pages of the English writer) and the wives and widows presiding like deposed queens at cavalry balls. Equally, Ford's use of campfire songs to punctuate his plotlines echoes Kipling's fondness for Cockney, aitch dropping barrack-room ballads as chapter-heads. (A few of Ford's titles, *My Darling Clementine, She Wore a Yellow Ribbon* and *When Johnny Comes Marching Home,* actually were titles of songs.)

But if, to an unmotivated eye and ear, Ford's cavalry romances look like so many animated Remington landscapes and sound like some of Kipling's gruffer and more sentimental fictions, somehow, by some alchemical process of which the cinema alone guards the secret, they add up to rather more than Kipling and Remington combined. It's a question, again, of the dancer and the dance. His finest work manifests so perfectly co-ordinated an amalgam of style and subject matter, of the vision and the thing seen, that the western trappings actually come to strike one as mere incidentals. It hardly matters, then, where these cavalrymen are bound. They are, in a sense, transfixed, arrested for ever in the realm of the symbolic. With Ford, you might say, *Destiny* Rides Again.

# 1952 The Band Wagon

How does one translate this image into print? One might, of course, write exclusively of Fred Astaire, not merely as a dancer (although he was, by well-nigh universal accord, one of the century's finest in any medium), not merely as a singer or actor or peerlessly debonair light comedian, but above all as the very epitome of *style* – style in the sense of Buffon's '*Le style est l'homme même*', style as an almost heraldic quality, bearing much the same relation to conventional attributes of 'stylishness' (that, in the American cinema, of a Franchot Tone or a Robert Montgomery) that the lions and wolves rampant on a coat-of-arms bear to living animals. Astaire, indeed, might have personified Style as other, medieval forms personified Chastity and Avarice.

The image in question is from Vincente Minnelli's musical comedy *The Band Wagon* and it's most probably a set photographer's still, not a frame enlargement from the film itself. But what makes other dancers stylish (a Gene Kelly, a Cyd Charisse) and only Fred Astaire the pure embodiment of Style is that, even if it were in fact a frame enlargement, *at no matter which point of the dance the image were arrested* (as anyone possessed of a tape of one of his musicals and a video freeze-frame button can instantly verify for himself) he would be frozen in a pose of supreme elegance, shrugging his feet as nonchalantly as if they were shoulders and exhibiting, at the choreography's transitional stages, none of those minor gestural infelicities, mostly imperceptible to the naked eye, to which one imagined even the greatest dancers had to be prone.

Equally, one might write of Vincente Minnelli, not merely as a director of musicals, not merely as a filmic choreographer, but above all as a 'stylist', the American cinema's most brilliant interior and, as my still demonstrates, exterior decorator. For it was the glory of the musical comedy that it could accord a director like Minnelli (or George Cukor, Stanley Donen, Charles Walters, George Sidney) a kind of artistic freedom denied him in his 'straight' films, except in so far as these resembled musicals, and rigorously denied all other American filmmakers – freedom in décor and costume, naturally, but also in camera movement and the exploration of cinematic space.

This is the paradox: that nothing so closely resembles a European art movie as an American musical. That fire-escape, for example, itself the colour of fire, that fire-escape zigzagging aslant the image as if it, too, like Astaire, were an abstraction, were the pure embodiment of Rhythm, where has it come from? *Film noir,* to be sure, in the first instance (the musical number is 'The Girl Hunt', a balletic parody of a Mickey Spillane novel); but then, the refined and urbanized *angst* of *film noir* itself derived from the warped perspectives and

looming shadows of prewar German Expressionism, from the cinema of
Murnau, Wiene, Lang, Arthur Robison and E. A. Dupont.

Similarly, it's not too farfetched to detect, in the showbiz Surrealism of
another of Minnelli's collaborations with Astaire, the portmanteau musical
confection *Ziegfeld Follies,* the influence, however trivialized, of the French
avant-gardists of the twenties, whereas in Europe such visual delirium, its power
of subversion preserved more or less intact, could be accommodated only by
unrepentantly non-generic – indeed, wilfully *sui generis* – films like Fellini's *8½*
and Resnais' *L'Année dernière à Marienbad.* Thus genre, too often lazily
compared to a straitjacket, should more properly be regarded as a type of
*uniform;* and, as with uniforms worn in the service of the Army, the Church and
the Law, a startlingly unrealistic, poetic and even peacocky surface may in
reality constitute a fundamental signifier of conformity. It's not after all by
chance that, for the whole of his professional life, Minnelli worked at Metro-
Goldwyn-Mayer, the nub of Hollywood's Establishment, its centre of gravity, so
to speak.

Gravity, though, isn't the word – not when, as in *The Band Wagon,* such
freedom is personified by perhaps the airiest spirit of the American cinema –
Astaire, a star on a stair.

117

# 1953 The Robe

Ta-da! Welcome, this prettily outfitted assembly of Romans seems to be saying to us, welcome to the wonderful world of CinemaScope!

Such an image, compositionally banal if numerically spectacular, does indeed conjure up an era, the mid-fifties, when the American cinema, in thrall to a manly, not to say macho, obsession with sheer size, deluded itself that its most effective weapons against television were enormous – and often outlandishly named – screen formats. CinemaScope, of which the British critic C. A. Lejeune wrote sniffily that it was 'like sitting inside a monstrous pillar box', was the first to be deployed in mainstream filmmaking (if one forgets that the wide screen had not only a history but a prehistory, whose most memorable manifestation, Abel Gance's triple-screen Polyvision of 1927, would transform his *Napoléon* into a three-ring circus). But there was also Cinerama (a word which, interestingly, is the exact anagram of 'American'), VistaVision (with its two Churchillian Vs), Technirama, WarnerScope, MetroScope, SuperScope, Panavision and Todd-AO. ('Todd' was the impresario Mike Todd, 'AO' stood for 'American Optical', and so overwhelming was the visual impact it felt more like *God*-AO. Todd was later responsible for SmelloVision, waggishly rechristened 'Todd-BO'.)

The fad for these formats eventually waned when it became clear that they offered no enduring threat to television: as ruthlessly squeezed on to the box as luggage into a bulging suitcase, there isn't one such 'blockbuster', from *South Pacific* to *2001*, that hasn't regularly turned up in the TV schedules. And, paradoxically, the only film I know which absolutely defies televisual adaptation is Eric Rohmer's *Le Rayon vert,* a modest art movie shot in a conventional, squarish ratio. In its closing scene the obstinately unforthcoming heroine, Delphine, is finally accorded the miracle she has been waiting for – the green ray, that last, fleeting and semi-mythical beam of a setting sun. Rohmer spent a year in a vain endeavour to capture the real phenomenon on film, before resigning himself to recreating it in the laboratory. And so minuscule is the flash of green that when the film is screened on television it proves to be completely invisible! There's a moral there somewhere.

In fact, *The Robe* was not the first CinemaScope film completed at Twentieth Century-Fox, the studio which initially took an option on the format. That was *How to Marry a Millionaire,* a brassy farce with Marilyn Monroe, amusing enough in its frivolous fashion but considered unseasonably trivial for the inauguration of the new technique. So *The Robe* was chosen instead, a turgidly bad movie, alas, but belonging to a genre, the pseudo-Biblical epic, which Hollywood has always taken comically seriously.

The snag is that Henry Koster, the man responsible for *The Robe,* was a

frankly hack director, and what was required for this most problematic of genres
was not a hack but a ham. In other words, Cecil B. DeMille, the Grandpa Moses
of the American cinema. For it *is* possible to admire the primitive, unrepentant
energy of DeMille's Biblical movies, even to regard him, as certain French critics
have done, as one of Hollywood's supreme storytellers. I don't know, though . . .
For I recall one of DeMille's epics, *Samson and Delilah*. I recall, as well, its two
leads, Victor Mature and Hedy Lamarr (of whom Groucho Marx said that he
didn't want to see a movie in which 'the man's tits are bigger than the
woman's'). I recall most vividly the scene in which Mature's Samson pulls down
the pillars of the Temple with the excruciating aplomb of a funfair strong man
ripping a telephone directory in half. And I guess, when it comes right down to
it, that I'm fonder of Hollywood when it's influenced by the sign of the dollar
than by the sign of the cross.

# 1954 Sansho dayu

## *Sansho the Bailiff*

The last scene of *Sansho dayu* is one of the most affecting in the history of the cinema. In medieval Japan a powerful family is disunited by its political adversaries: the father is exiled, the children enslaved, the mother sold into prostitution. As it proceeds, however, the narrative appears to be gravitating towards a climactic reunion between the one surviving child, a son, and his mother (or a woman who may or may not be his mother). Their reunion, when it finally does take place, occurs on an isolated beach on which the woman in question, a blind hag, is gathering driftwood. The young man approaches her. The bewildered old woman gingerly extends a hand and runs her fingertips over the dips and acclivities of his face. He *is* her son; she, unrecognizable as she is, blind as she is, *is* his mother. Whereupon, taking its departure from the scene with a slow panning shot of heartrending beauty, the camera rises up and refocuses on a peasant who is serenely tilling his field not far off: this, not the embrace of mother and son, is the film's closing shot, the shot that one carries away from the cinema. The reunion so longed for, by us as much as by the characters themselves, has passed as hauntingly unheeded by the rest of the world as the lonely fall of Icarus in Breughel's painting of that title.

As a general rule, I would say that the films which mean most to me, and to which I return (if only in my mind) again and again, are those of which one element alone is beautiful, a single formal or stylistic parameter which contrives to determine, as a symptom rather than a syndrome, my perception of the filmic material in its entirety (e.g. Bresson, Marguerite Duras, the Straubs). In Kenji Mizoguchi's cinema *everything* is beautiful: the landscapes are breathtaking; the faces are photogenically eloquent; the camera movements are fluid and complex; the black-and-white (more precisely, black-and-silver) cinematography is subtle and dense of texture; the compositions are so precise it's as if space itself were being cut along a dotted line. It's a form of beauty, however, that never precludes the effective recreation of a world in which evil and ugliness exist. In the scene illustrated opposite (and in which one first notices the beauty of the faces, of the kimonos, not least of the hats, those basic vestmentary signifiers of Mizoguchi's films, just as samurai masks are of Kurosawa's), the fleeing family has reached a river bank. The tips of tall rushes sway in the foreground; there is a hint of elegantly elongated skiffs in the distance. For us Westerners, beyond the immediate narrative circumstance, such a shot represents a quintessence of Japanese decorative art, worthy of any of the great printmakers. Imagine our dismay, then, when the mother (the brilliant actress Kinoyu Tanaka) delivers a

line of dialogue to her children which a subtitle translates as (and I quote from memory): 'Oh, let's move away! It's so sinister here.' Sinister? But it's *exquisite*! And yet, when we look more closely, it dawns on us that she's right. It's both sinister (as setting) and exquisite (as cinema). That was the secret of Mizoguchi, as it was of Hokusai, whose ineffably luscious Wave was, after all, a tidal wave.

Although one of the world's oldest, and richest in masterpieces, the Japanese cinema was not 'discovered' by the West until 1951, when Akira Kurosawa's *Rashomon* was premièred at the Venice Festival. And, even when once internationally established, it was Kurosawa, then Ozu, then, from a younger generation, Oshima on whom most attention would focus. For all but genuine *cinéphiles* Mizoguchi has remained little more than a name, the director at most of a single film, *Ugetsu Monogatari*, to whom and which lip service, but rarely more than lip service, has been paid. Yet he was, indisputably, one of the greatest practitioners of pure *mise-en-scène* the cinema has ever known and the master of the heroically sustained long take. And, as with *Oharu, Yang Kwei-Fei, Shin Heike Monogatari* and so many of his works, *Sansho dayu* is one of those films *for whose sake the cinema exists* – just as it perhaps exists for the sake of its own last scene.

# 1955 Lola Montès

Jacques Demy named his first film, *Lola*, after her and dedicated it to her creator, Max Ophüls. The English-born critic David Thomson has written persuasively of the turntable on which poor Lola pivots amid the gaudy trappings of a circus ring as the apotheosis of Ophüls' sensitivity to the tensions and transience of circularity – the spiral staircases of *Letter From an Unknown Woman*, the trio of Maupassant tales from *Le Plaisir*, the earrings passing from hand to hand in *Madame de . . .* and of course the merry-go-round (or maybe melancholy-go-round) of *La Ronde*. (The deviser of the longest, most sinuous, most circuitous tracking-shot *sentences* in the history of the cinema, Ophüls was the only director who could successfully have adapted Proust.) Another critic, the American Andrew Sarris, fantasized whimsically that, at Ophüls' death, all the dolly cameras in the world would have bowed as one in tribute to his memory. And another (if, at this stage of his life, only aspiring) director, the young François Truffaut, one of the film's most unconditional champions – he proudly confessed to having seen it five times during the first week of its initial release – referred to it, in a near-blasphemous reference to Joan of Arc, as 'Lola at the Stake'. *Lola Montès* is, in other words, a cult film.

Why so? Naturally, as all cult films demand (except for certain contemporary examples by such fashionable filmmakers as David Lynch, Luc Besson and Quentin Tarantino, whose cultishness, like a production value, is meticulously pre-programmed into the original project), it was both shot and shown against a background of hostility and philistinism. Considered, for so expensive a film, too long and too complex of structure – but, as with all long films, the spectator has to learn to pace himself like an athlete, just as the director and his cast must have done during the shoot – it was mangled by its producers and remained visible for decades only in a crude, re-edited version. Naturally, too, as Ophüls' very last film (he died of a heart attack in 1957), it has been pounced upon by fetishist *cinéphiles* ghoulishly avid for 'testaments' (Ford's *Seven Women*, Dreyer's *Gertrud*, Renoir's *Le Petit Théâtre de Jean Renoir*, and so on).

But it goes somewhat deeper than that. For all the charm of its setting (and it's possible to regret that the whole film doesn't take place inside the circus tent, minus the conventional openings-out to Lola's earlier life, her affairs with Ludwig I of Bavaria, Franz Liszt, etc.), for all the breathtaking cranes and pans, tilts and tracks, which make this, in the sense of the term as it refers to cartoons, the most brilliantly *animated* of CinemaScope movies, and for all the euphoria that Ophüls' palatial settings cannot help but generate in the spectator, *Lola Montès* is a strangely sombre, even a heartbreaking, film. Truffaut was right. The sex object personified, enthroned in her golden cage, revolving as pointlessly

as a guinea pig on a treadmill, Lola (played, in the sole highlight of her dreary sexpot's career, by Martine Carol, an actress whose chronic behavioural impassivity suggests she took the word 'statuesque', often used to describe her very unkittenish allure, a mite too literally), is ultimately forced to remove, not the canonic seven veils, but the eighth, that which conceals the soul. She may have been a whore rather than a virgin, but the film's great central metaphor, after all, a metaphor flagrant in the image above, with its candles and chapels and chandeliers, with its light and tinselly Gothic arches, is of the circus as cathedral, of striptease as ritual.

Truffaut was right, too, about Ophüls' own stature (and his importance in the fifties, a basically stagnant and regressive period for the European cinema). *Lola Montès* has survived. The film has been restored. It's posterity which has had the final cut.

# 1956 Beyond a Reasonable Doubt

Two men sitting in an automobile. Two men outfitted in the felt hats and boxy, double-breasted suits and soberly immaculate collars and ties that, for most of us, have come to evoke the Hollywood cinema of the thirties, forties and fifties rather than any real, still recollectable time or place. This photograph, I admit, isn't 'interesting'; its composition isn't eye-fetching; it might have served indiscriminately to epitomize scores of thrillers and dramas and police procedural movies made in Hollywood between, let's say, 1930 and 1960. Precisely. For it's perhaps time to acknowledge the extent to which the textural specificity of the American cinema is contingent upon what might be called its 'urbanality'. Putting it more crudely, it's all very well talking about *The Ten Commandments* and *Gone With the Wind* and *Casablanca* and *Rio Bravo*, but what going to the cinema during those years really meant was watching near-identical men in near-identical suits and hats sitting in near-identical apartment rooms and bars and black, bulbous automobiles; was watching movies that were, paradoxically, like nothing so much as books – books without illustrations. And therein, in a way which is difficult to communicate to the uninitiated but which no true *cinéphile* will ever need to have explained, can be found the medium's metallic poetry.

The film in question is Fritz Lang's *Beyond a Reasonable Doubt* and the two men are Sidney Blackmer and Dana Andrews. Its plot is exactly that – a plot – hatched by the newspaper publisher played by Blackmer and the journalist played by Andrews, a plot whereby the latter will deliberately implicate himself in an unsolved murder in order to demonstrate the ease with which circumstantial evidence can lead to wrongful conviction. There is, I should add, an eleventh-hour twist; but it's a twist only until the instant it's revealed; in the very next instant one realizes that the film could not have ended any other way. Jacques Rivette called it a theorem, a *tabula rasa*. It is, in any event, the rigorous purification of a genre to which Lang and certain of his fellow émigrés, Robert Siodmak, Billy Wilder, Otto Preminger and Edgar Ulmer, had given of their best: the *film noir*.

There is, though, a most curious paradox in the *film noir*. I yield to no one, as they say, in my love of the genre and I recognize the pertinence of much that has been written about its inherent pessimism. Yet I must confess to never having found that pessimism very convincing. No one in the forties ever went to see a *film noir* with a sense that he was about to submit to a harrowing but salutary dose of existential nihilism (a nihilism that isn't just a matter of critical interpretation but is quite perceptible in both narrative detail and visual texture), just as no one ever need recoil from watching one on television now. *Films noirs*

are great fun, for God's sake, great fun primarily because they never really do persuade one that the despair that they portray is ultimately a truth of the human condition – in the way that, at least while one is experiencing it, a film by Bergman does, or a novel by Kafka, or an opera by Berg. For most of us, I suspect, their fabled negativity is precisely that: a *negative* (in the photographic sense of the word) of the fundamental American positivity and optimism. The people who made them (and who were usually, as I've said, European exiles) loved America, just as did the people who watched them. Secretly, I believe, *they were not even meant to convince.*

*Beyond a Reasonable Doubt*, however, *was* meant to convince. As has seldom been the case in Hollywood's history, it's a film, a visually drab and unyielding film, *about absolutely nothing else but its own subject.* Two men in hats and suits sit in an automobile and hatch a plot, two men whose white faces and crisp white shirts stand out against the enveloping darkness like the white chalkings of a mathematical formula on a blackboard, a *tableau noir.*

# 1957 Soshun

## *Early Spring*

The titles are frequently seasonal and, in translation, easily confused: *Late Spring, Early Spring, Late Autumn, The End of Summer, An Autumn Afternoon*. Or else, to a Western ear, they sound almost parodically 'Japanese': *A Story of Floating Weeds, The Flavour of Green Tea Over Rice, Equinox Flower* and *Floating Weeds* a second time. Or else they employ a curious and slightly precious semantic construction, one that was possibly unique to Ozu, involving the conjunction 'but' succeeded by three tantalizing suspension points: *I Graduated, But . . ., I Flunked, But . . .,* even *I Was Born, But . . .* Or else they foreground the name of Japan's capital city, as in *Tokyo Chorus, A Tokyo Woman, An Inn in Tokyo, Tokyo Story* and *Twilight in Tokyo*.

As for the films themselves, the most tenacious critical cliché on their subject, a cliché endorsed even by those (rare) critics who know and admire the oeuvre, is that they are 'all the same' – calm, introspective comedy-dramas of family life, of the transience yet, equally, the immutability of everything that profoundly matters in a human existence. Received wisdom has it, too, that their overall visual style, a style instantly identifiable from a single frame from any one film, tends to be confined to a series of static, waist-level, medium-distance shots (the films' characters are frequently cross-legged) of homely domestic, office or bar interiors, the latter with a genteel hint of neon in the middle distance, and usually, in the late colour films, of a faint, unaggressively metal-green tonality. For Westerners, in consequence, Yasujiro Ozu is the most Japanese of Japanese directors.

All of which, at least up to a point, is true. Yet many of his early productions were genre movies, thrillers, burlesque comedies and baroque Sternbergian melodramas. There is also the paradoxical fact that the textual consistency of his best-known films, both in subject-matter and in compositional style (and even in his choice of performers), grants a Western spectator easier access to them than would otherwise be possible. Just as we bring to the vision of most English or American movies a set of sociocultural preconceptions and predispositions which the filmmaker himself is thereby free to assume as a given on our part, so, if we have already seen a couple of Ozu's films, we feel we already know these people, their homes, their offices and their bars, and we don't have to start from scratch with every new work. Finally, I sometimes fancied, while writing this book, that it might be fun to have its index consist exclusively of key film titles which ought to have been, but actually were *not,* cited in the text itself; and, if such an index were to have been drawn up, it would doubtless have had to include every single Ozu

film (or all those, certainly, that I have seen: several of the early works seem not to have survived). Until the late sixties, when his name would first become conjurable, film culture in the West had appeared to manage quite well without Ozu. Once he had been 'discovered', it was impossible to ignore him.

With the extreme tenderness that he would display towards each of his characters, Ozu is, in fact, irresistible. And if, ultimately, he strikes us as less 'difficult' than any other Japanese director, it's perhaps a question of what is called off-screen space. Although neglected by Anglo-American critics, off-screen space (which is to say, that invisible but implicit context of a film beyond the camera's field of vision) is one of the most significant concepts of cinema theory. It can be envisaged in very general terms (the Holocaust, for example, as the off-screen space of *Schindler's List*) or within a narrower social framework (being what, speculatively, happens downstairs in James Ivory's *The Remains of the Day* when the on-screen action is taking place upstairs, and vice versa); it may defy speculation altogether (the off-screen space of a Godard film is simply unimaginable) or it may pose genuine cultural challenges, as with, precisely, the alleged 'obscurity', for Western spectators, of Japanese films, an obscurity deriving less from what is explicit on-screen than what is implicit off.

If Ozu's films, ultra-Japanese as they are, pose surprisingly few problems of this nature, it's surely that, such is their humanity, such their universality, their off-screen space is the world itself, the world in which all of us have to live.

# 1958 Jalsaghar
## *The Music Room*

It was the young and impertinently iconoclastic journalist François Truffaut who walked out of a Cannes Festival screening of Satyajit Ray's *Pather Panchali* with the cavalierly blunt comment that 'I don't want to see a film about Indian peasants'. This was of course reprehensibly racist and patronizing of him (his arrogance slightly extenuated by the fact that Ray was an unknown quantity in 1956). And yet . . . It's surely one of the functions of the critic to, if one may say, cut through the crap, the 'crap' in this instance being the idea that European or American *cinéphiles*, when once installed inside a cinema auditorium, become non-racist almost by definition and are as deliriously pleased to be watching a film about an impoverished community in rural India as one about dinosaurs rampaging through a theme park, let's say, or another about what the butler *didn't* see in an English Home Counties mansion in the nineteen-thirties. As we all know, even if no one dares to admit it, this is simply not true. Most of us Westerners in fact are still, like Truffaut in the fifties, not all that tremendously keen on films about Indian (or African or Chinese or Latin American) peasants. And even if we do succeed in motivating ourselves, there will always be a last, lingering vestige of Eurocentric resistance to be overcome, a resistance whose inherently racist essence we try to camouflage by airy, disingenuously neutral allusions to the formal and stylistic shortcomings of a 'primitive' culture.

*Pace* the late Truffaut, however, it was one of the achievements of Satyajit Ray that by virtue of his debuting trilogy of films (*Pather Panchali, Aparajito, The World of Apu*) he contrived almost immediately, and for the period almost single-handedly, to surmount such a resistance. (Not for the French, though, who began to appreciate his work only in the eighties and nineties: Truffaut's influence as an arbiter of taste cannot be overestimated.) *Panchali* was an implausible triumph at Cannes, that weird mélange of stock exchange, circus ring and court of miracles. And, with his following film, *The Music Room*, manifesting an unexpected sophistication of style and technique, Ray confirmed that he could no longer be filed away in the ungrateful and condescending category of 'Third World humanist', complete with the raw granularity of photographic texture typical of that kind of filmmaker and which paradoxically obscures the very imagery it has generated. He would subsequently make comedies and dramas, fairy-tales and message movies, costumed fantasies and contemporary social satires. He would become, in short, a filmmaker like any other.

*The Music Room* is, as it happens, one of his least overtly 'humanist' works, a

slow, contemplative study of a slow, contemplative man, a man who endeavours to keep the twentieth century at bay by devoting what energy he still possesses to the restoration, to its former, colonialist splendour, and for one last, spectral concert, of his villa's crumbling music room. And there is, present in this film, as in the shot I have selected from it, the trope, the behavioural motif, or whatever one cares to call it, that has above all others remained with me from a lifetime of viewing Satyajit Ray's work: I mean the amazing absence in his films of *meaningful ambulation*. Ray's characters, his male characters mostly but by no means exclusively, are so very horizontal! Horizontal from the heat, to be sure, as from the tetchy, fly-ridden enervation that it induces, but horizontal, too, as if in their very *souls*. They seldom walk. They never run. Ray almost always portrays them limp and languorous on a couch, fanning themselves if no servant can be mustered to fan them.

Is this what is termed a theme? Is it, in other words, what Ray's work is ultimately 'about'? Or is it just India? The faintly caricatural symbol of an etiolated Indian middle-class? And is it important in his work (it is, as I say, its most indelible afterimage for me personally) or is it as peculiar, yet equally as incidental, to it as the frequency of semi-colons in Shakespeare's plays?

I am not a racist and I have seen practically all of Ray's films – yet, somehow, alas, the twain never have quite met.

# 1959  A bout de souffle

## *Breathless*

Study this shot from Jean-Luc Godard's *A bout de souffle,* a shot which is now, astoundingly, thirty-six years old: the Gauloise clenched between Jean-Paul Belmondo's fleshy, insolent lips, his rakish tweed cap, his dark glasses, his striped shirt unbuttoned at the cuffs, his white Calvin Kleinish boxer shorts and matching white socks, the telephone, the tripod and, in an apartment that is otherwise bare, the two independently signifying surfaces of the little volume on Picasso and the pinned-up snapshot of a cover girl.

Aside from no more than a couple of insignificant items (the telephone and the record-player), the photograph could have been taken yesterday for *Esquire* or *Vanity Fair*. And if Godard's critical stock has fallen of late, the truth is that, as one of the century's supreme inventors of forms, his genius has been usurped by its own posterity. Moreover, the evidence that not merely the cinema *but the world itself* has become Godardian is staring us all in the face.

It was Godard who first conceived of editing as the art of discontinuity rather than continuity; Godard who first paid retrospective homage to the long neglected icons of popular culture; Godard who first understood that cinema was whatever was projected on a screen, becoming the medium's Tinteretto of television, its Leonardo da video; Godard who first proposed that the filmic image had to be flattened out for the sake of its own autonomy, that, as long as perspective persisted, the image would remain inferior to, because ultimately imitative of, what we term 'reality'; and it was Godard who first foresaw that the image would eventually dethrone the word as the irreducible unit of communication. (McLuhan, the other major theorist of such a semantic displacement, continued to have recourse to words to describe the end of the Word, whereas Godard used images and, if words, then words *as* images.)

If, nowadays, these innovations are a commonplace of the cinema (and of the media in general), it's by virtue of Godard's example. In the movies of self-styled stylists like Besson, Beineix and Carax his legendary fertility of imagination may have been reduced to a rash of superficial tics, but he made them possible nevertheless. Would *Annie Hall* have been filmed in quite the same manner if Godard's poisoned Valentines to Anna Karina had not provided the model? Would Robert De Niro's Brando-inspired 'I coulda been a contender' monologue in *Raging Bull* have been imaginable without Belmondo's ironic, affectionate mimicry of Bogart in *A bout de souffle?*

Or consider a famous shot from *Deux ou trois choses que je sais d'elle*. The film's heroine (Marina Vlady) is stirring a *café au lait* in her apartment when

Godard brusquely switches to an overhead close-up, transforming an anfractuous whorl of coffee and milk into a diminutive cosmos – a visual conceit that, if unprecedented in 1967, would scarcely raise an eyebrow these days in a TV commercial for Gold Blend. Yet there is nothing inherently shocking in the notion of Godard's cosmic apprehension becoming the mere fodder of advertising. In the twenties, after all, the revolutionary thrust of Cubism eventually degenerated into the *art déco* stylistics of a Dubonnet poster.

Godard's intuitions, moreover, have been recuperated and domesticated not only by TV commercials but, in the systematic way in which it pulverizes both its own matter and meaning, by television itself, as similarly by video promos, billboards, newspaper and magazine layouts, restaurant décors, the lettering of logos and trademarks, computer graphics, comic-strip art, fashion photography, even by the negligent drop-dead chic with which a mannequin swishes down a catwalk, her hair swaying as languidly as Karina's in *Une femme est une femme*. Indeed, well-nigh everything which articulates our contemporary urban existence, our 'universe of persuasion', as Jean Baudrillard has described it, can be traced back, directly or indirectly, to Godard's work. We now 'shoot' the world, in short, in just the way he has always shot his films.

# 1960 Le Testament d'Orphée
## *The Testament of Orpheus*

In 1972 the American director Richard Fleischer made a diverting science-fiction movie, *The Fantastic Voyage* – diverting in its premise, I should say, almost wholly botched, alas, in its execution. The premise in question was that of an exploratory voyage, taken by a miniaturized team of doctors in a correspondingly miniature submarine, through the insides of an atomic scientist who has suffered brain damage in the wake of an assassination attempt. And the botched execution derived from Hollywood's formulary insistence on a 'real' plot, complete with conventional romantic relief (as one refers to 'comic relief'), an eleventh-hour deliverance and, above (or below) all, the presence inside the patient's body of what might be termed an *antibody,* a villain, a baddie, an atheistic fifth columnist in the pay of an unspecified, albeit easily inferable, 'foreign power', who enjoys nothing so much as ragging his piously Christian colleagues. 'Let me know,' he sneers, 'when we reach the soul.'

Jean Cocteau's *envoi* to the cinema, *Le Testament d'Orphée* (Orpheus himself, by the way, is entirely marginal to the film's narrative and is foregrounded in its title as the poet's patented trademark, his logo, his watermark, exactly, perhaps, what Mickey Mouse was to Disney's output), also constituted an exploratory voyage around the inside of an individual – but one which did in fact reach his soul. *Le Testament d'Orphée* is (for the cinema) that extremely rare artefact, a Protean projection of selfhood, not so much a film as *a man who has turned himself into a film,* who has, by some inexplicable Orphic and metamorphic process, been transformed into a work of art. So much so that, when one enters the cinema, one has the impression (precisely as did the miniaturized surgeons of *The Fantastic Voyage*) that one is also entering a genius's brain; and, for any spectator unadmiring of Cocteau himself, indifferent or hostile to his aesthetic persona, there is absolutely nothing remaining in the film, neither a plot point nor a performance, not a single 'uncoctelian' element, with which it's possible to engage.

I said above that Cocteau's example was rare, but it's not quite unique. As filmic 'testaments', displaying varying degrees of autobiographical and sometimes frankly solipsistic self-referentiality, one might equally cite Fellini's *8½,* Wajda's *Everything For Sale,* Sturges' *Sullivan's Travels,* Dziga-Vertov's *The Man with a Movie Camera,* Truffaut's *La Nuit américaine,* Powell's *Peeping Tom,* Kurosawa's *Dreams,* Joris Ivens' *Une histoire de vent,* Paradzhanov's *Sayat Nova,* Wenders' *The State of Things,* Duras's *Le Camion,* Bergman's *Now About All These Women,* Terence Davies' *The Long Day*

*Closes*, Lang's *Die Tausend Augen des Dr. Mabuse*, Tarkovski's *Mirror* and virtually anything by Godard. These are all films which exploit, to borrow the English-language title of Truffaut's, a metaphysical equivalent of 'day for night' in order to expose the tenebrosity of the soul to the light.

In Cocteau's case, moreover, such total control operates on every single level of the film's discourse, even that of a publicity still. Study our illustration. Here is Cocteau such as into himself, as Mallarmé famously wrote of Poe, Eternity has transformed him. Here he is, dying on film. (He would die in life, as it were, just three years later.) Here, too, is that unmistakable vestimentary 'look' that one recalls from a score of scribbled self-portraits: the canary-yellow suede jacket with its cuffs folded back over the wrists, the V-neck pullover, the knotted silk tie, the gold pinkie ring encircling the elegantly elongated, cigarette-slim finger. Every crease, too, on the sheet on which he is stretched out has been invested with the witty, seductive linearity of his own graphic style. This photograph, in short, is not a photograph at all but a Cocteau drawing which has turned itself into a photograph.

# 1961 L'Année dernière à Marienbad
## *Last Year at Marienbad*

Perhaps – or should I say doubtless – to be honest, I don't actually know – despite the atrocity of the offence – perhaps (I say) – it's possible – it just might have been preferable – almost any trite and unresonant word finds itself, in this spa, in this *ville d'eau*, imbued with the allure of a password, a word of honour, the very Word of God. In this spa, this garden – a symmetrically organized French garden designed to serve as the 'front', as the smooth and respectable façade, for the criminal activities of its roots – is inscribed a triangle as anxiety-inducing as one of Chirico's set-squares. But why? And these figures, who stand immobile on the garden path like so many chessmen and chesswomen, why do they cast shadows when the trees aligning the path do not? Yes, the shadows have been painted on, but why, for heaven's sake? And whose idea was it that chess pieces themselves, to while away the time between moves, surreptitiously play a little game with matchsticks called Nim, a game that bears a curious structural resemblance to the mental processes of the two players sitting opposite each other, with the spa spread out across their knees like a chessboard?

The chess players I refer to were the Alains Resnais and Robbe-Grillet, respectively the director and scenarist of *Last Year at Marienbad*. Shot in black-and-white, in an extravagantly oblong CinemaScope format that made every one of its images as elegant as a tuxedo, it was probably the very last film (to date) around which a scandal arose by virtue of its style alone rather than its subject matter (as would subsequently be the case with Rivette's *La Religieuse*, Pasolini's *Salò* and Scorsese's *The Last Temptation of Christ* among others). *Marienbad*, then, was that prodigy, a genuinely avant-garde film (its plot? A man meets a woman at a spa and puts it to her that they might have had an affair the year before either at the same spa or at another or possibly at neither) that prompted a debate *solely* because it was avant-garde.

One of the defining, albeit least frequently observed, properties of the avant-garde in any medium, though, is the smoke-screen that it wilfully throws up (in the short-term at least) over its own origins and antecedents, over the roots of its dream, so to speak, tending to leave the impression that it owes nothing to anyone, each of its products having hatched out of its own self as pristinely as Clytemnestra out of her egg. Yet it is, this avant-garde, or rather was, a datable historical moment of twentieth-century culture, and its works can be seen to be more intimately interconnected than is true of many a more superficially coherent genre. So it is with *Last Year at Marienbad*.

By Resnais' own account, the film's laminated interactions of time and memory were a direct consequence of his fascination with a revolutionary flashback in Cocteau's *Orphée* which dispensed with all the commonplace symptoms of such a device: the rippling screen, the hushed voice-off, and so on; and it's from Cocteau's film, too, from the poetic aplomb with which it transfixed human figures within a codified and nearly abstract setting, that can be traced *Marienbad's* eerie, stylish hieraticism. Beyond Cocteau, though, Resnais succeeded at last in reconciling Feuillade, the artisan, the Douanier Rousseau of Surrealist cinema, with L'Herbier, the aesthete, who despised Feuillade and whose formal mastery was the equal of Resnais' own, just as L'Herbier's famous white gloves might be compared to Resnais' often photographed parka with its tufted fur collar and his viewfinder dangling on his pullover as elegantly as a monocle. And, like L'Herbier (in *L'Argent*), Resnais installed at the core of his mystery a supernaturally ethereal and voguish vamp, the unforgettable Delphine Seyrig, who didn't have to do much more than graciously permit the camera to soak her up.

Is *Last Year at Marienbad* a masterpiece? Perhaps – or should I say doubtless – to be honest, I don't actually know.

# 1962 Lawrence of Arabia

Sir David Lean was, with his contemporaries Sir Carol Reed and Sir Laurence Olivier, one of the three august director-knights (as one refers to actor-knights) of the British cinema. Not that, in the thirties and forties, when first heard of, any of these names was so prestigiously prefixed; yet knighthood must always have appeared a foregone conclusion. Theirs was a cinema By Appointment, as there are marmalades and cornflakes and deerstalker hats By Appointment. Indelibly academic in texture, if by no means wanting in visual grace or narrative verve, Lean's films in particular differed from the industry's more conventional products (of a sometimes slightly fey introversion, it has to be said) not least in the ambassadorial confidence with which they projected fitting – which tended to mean 'flattering' – images of Britain around the globe.

But if he became the unrivalled master of what might be called 'the well-made film' (on the model of the well-made play, from Pinero to Rattigan), if the unfaltering technical maestria of his finest work could on occasion degenerate into a cold, finicky perfectionism for which the now pejorative term of 'academic' seems not too harsh a word (perfectionism without perfection, a dispiriting mode of artistry), such a qualification has to be qualified in its turn by the acknowledgement that, for numerous disciples, Lean's work *was* the Academy. One may not necessarily care for what he did; but what he did, he did better than any of his imitators. And, especially in recent years, imitators of Lean have abounded, from Spielberg (the scenes of pure spectacle in *Empire of the Sun* and *Schindler's List*) via the school of British directors presided over by David Puttnam (Roland Joffé's *The Killing Fields* and *The Mission,* Hugh Hudson's *Greystoke* and *Revolution,* Michael Caton-Jones' *Memphis Belle*) to the flatulent confections of that other director-knight, Sir Richard Attenborough (*Gandhi* and *Cry Freedom*). Lean's influence on their work is patent not merely in their choice of subject matter and often self-consciously epic attitude to *mise-en-scène* but also in the manner in which their films apotheosize the planet's great elemental spaces, just as his own in later years would do: the jungle (*The Bridge on the River Kwai*), the desert (*Lawrence of Arabia*), the steppes (*Doctor Zhivago*), the ocean (*Ryan's Daughter*), the mountains (*A Passage to India*) and the sky (all of the above).

Of these there remains but one indisputable masterpiece: the perverse and fascinating *Lawrence*. Perhaps because, like his dreamily equivocal hero, Lean himself 'went native', himself became enamoured of the desert, of the glinting harmonies of sun and sand and steel, the British cinema's waspish, white-haired Silver Prince contrived for once to throw off the ungrateful mantle of 'brilliant technician', a label which had clung to him from his very first film, and

surrendered completely, even obsessively, to his material.

That it was an obsession can be seen in the image reproduced above (one of many, one of practically any, that I could have chosen from the film), for nothing but obsession, surely, could have elicited from a man like Lean such an exultant crucifix, such a pale, blond, eroticized English Christ, such a vast blue sun of a sky. It's an image, indeed, whose reproduction (as is very seldom the case) would be unthinkable in any but a miniaturization of the cinematic format whose elongated contours it embraces. For where other, frequently gifted, filmmakers were content to exploit the wide screen as a strictly technical enhancement (and there were those, of course, no less gifted, who resisted it as a technical impoverishment), it was Lean's genius to have perceived in Panavision the potential of, precisely, a panoramic vision, a *horizon*.

# 1963 The Nutty Professor

This image represents what might be called a test case. Not a test (for the moment at least) of your tolerance of Jerry Lewis, nor of the problematic notion that a film entitled *The Nutty Professor* merits inclusion in a book whose aim is to celebrate the centenary of the cinema. It's a test, no less, of your appreciation, indeed your love, of the medium itself. For if it's possible, even easy, to dislike Jerry Lewis, possible to dislike *The Nutty Professor,* possible, too, to judge the image opposite as kitschy, downright ugly, I would nevertheless submit that, if you cannot understand how such an image might *ever* be judged beautiful, even as it rejects, or insults, every virtue in the canon of high-art pictorialism, if you cannot understand how its garish colour tonality, so very vulgar on the printed page, may be transfigured within the context of the medium to which it owes allegiance, then you do not understand the cinema.

It is, I fear, a matter of faith. No doubt about it, Jerry Lewis and Stella Stevens inhabit a wholly different universe from Eve Francis on that lonely road to nowhere or Eisenstein's elegant, murderous Tsarist soldiery. So can Jerry and Stella, too, be Art? For heaven's sake, how can Jerry Lewis be Art? Doesn't it smack just a tad of the Fordist (Henry, not John) assembly line when a film looks as new, as indecently streamlined, as a new car or kitchen unit? And yet, exactly as if a *Saturday Evening Post* cover by Norman Rockwell were to be exhibited in the Prado, where its usurped prominence would take some getting used to, but, once you had got used to it, why yes, *yes!* it didn't seem at all incongruous beside the El Grecos and the Goyas and the Velasquezes, just so does Mantra-like contemplation of goofy, buck-toothed Jerry and his web of candy-coloured beakers start to prompt untoward stirrings in the *cinéphile*'s vitals. At which point another auteurist is born.

And Jerry himself? Even if, over the last three decades, grudgingly or enthusiastically, the Anglo-American film-critical Establishment has inherited from its Parisian confrères the virtual rewriting of cinema history – most notably, the rehabilitation of the mainstream Hollywood product and the apotheosis of the director as auteur – it has elected to *draw the line* at Jerry Lewis, with the Americans taking especial exception to being harangued on how they ought to interpret their own culture.

So who's right? It all depends on what you want from the cinema. The fact is that, as a director (and this is a rarer phenomenon than is usually supposed and almost unheard-of in Hollywood), Jerry Lewis is an *auteur complet,* a filmmaker exercising such autocratic control over every single aspect of his films (which he writes, directs and stars in) that, were he to drop dead during a shoot, he could not conceivably be replaced by some competent, available craftsman. The fact is,

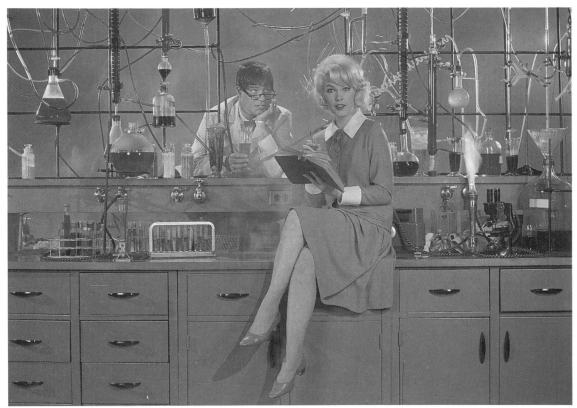

too, that, as a performer, the demented, double-jointed kineticism of his routines not merely links him with a long and prestigious tradition of manic, non-verbal burlesque, from Harry Langdon to Harpo Marx (who has always been *the* Marx Brother for French spectators, rather than Groucho), but also exposes and exploits one of the fundamental mainsprings of filmic slapstick – what psychoanalysts term 'the return of the repressed'. From the psyche of the on-screen 'Jerry' have been removed, as one might remove the little auxiliary side wheels of an infant's bicycle, all those checks and balances which allow us to live as reasonably functioning social beings. Liberated from these props, he regresses into the squeaking and squawking, disarticulated, licentious and incontinent creature for whom British and American critics have had such vocal distaste.

Confronted with their squeamishness, the French, for their part, would no doubt retort that the unconscious is never a pretty sight (which is why it's repressed in the first place) and point out to unrepentant sceptics that the schizophrenia of his character in *The Nutty Professor* proved just how alert Lewis has after all been to the implications of his persona. As to whether the unrelenting frenzy generated by this release of latent psychic energy is actually amusing in an enjoyable kind of way, there the critic is obliged to abdicate from his role as adviser. With Jerry Lewis, ultimately, you are on your own.

# 1964 Gertrud

The eponymous heroine of Carl Theodor Dreyer's last film, *Gertrud* (based on a proto-feminist Swedish play from the late teens of the century), is a fortyish woman who, having rejected with a strange, serene contempt the emotional and spiritual compromises that are all her husband and her lover alike have to offer her, reconciles herself, with resignation and grace, to the total solitude which will for ever after be the consequence of her intransigence. It's a film on which a great deal might be written (and has been written), but there's one moment in its narrative that particularly interests me: the moment when Gertrud, played by Nina Pens Rode, gets up from the divan on which she has been sitting and takes a few steps towards the door. As she does so, the camera, which has had her framed in a medium shot, tilts slightly upward to accommodate her erect form.

What's so interesting about that? you might ask. Nothing, if not precisely its lack of interest, its exclusively *utilitarian* quality as a camera movement. To the extent that it has one, *Gertrud*'s popular reputation is of a film cramped and constricted by its own headache-inducing formalism; a stately, even stodgy film in which shot follows shot in accordance with a heroically sustained but externally imposed logic; a film, in short, whose creator is just too ethereal, too otherworldly, to stoop to showing us, clearly and simply, what his characters might be up to. Yet what that single shot in *Gertrud* enables us to understand is that Dreyer's films are both magical *and* functional, and that the famous formalism is often simply a question of *trompe-l'oeil*.

How so? It is, perhaps, because his images are generated not by any ambition to make pretty pictures but by a desire to disinter the truth, a truth at once physical and metaphysical, at their core. In the disinterment of that truth a visual gift, an *eye*, is a crucial but not a primary factor – not a prerequisite but what I would call a *postrequisite*. Its disinterment is contingent, rather, on how Dreyer reflects on the image he is about to create rather than on what the image he has created reflects back into his camera lens; on his capacity to look inwardly not outwardly; on the fact, supremely, that cinematic vision is a matter more of the eyes one possesses than of what there is in front of them. Attitude, here, is altitude.

Perhaps *Gertrud* is beyond criticism – criticism still has to catch up with it. On its release, it was widely viewed as an embarrassing coda to an exemplary career, a pitiable manifestation of 'senilia', as we refer to juvenilia. With a handful of exceptions, the world's critics (who should have their inner eye tested every five years or so) were not even prepared to *wager* on Dreyer, to assume that the man who made *La Passion de Jeanne d'Arc* and *Ordet* might just know what he was doing, that, like Ford's *Seven Women*, Renoir's *Le Petit Théâtre de Jean Renoir*

and Bresson's *L'Argent, Gertrud* might just be one of those autumnal masterpieces by which several of the cinema's geniuses have taken their leave of the medium (and whose peculiar glow is comparable to the last, unexpectedly green, ray of a setting sun). These critics, now, have virtually all gone; *Gertrud* survives. It was ever thus.

The film was released in 1964. And, on the critical front, things have only got worse. A whole new generation of reviewers has arisen for whom, with the odd, entirely predictable exception (basically, *Citizen Kane*), the history of the cinema began with Scorsese's *Mean Streets* and Coppola's *The Godfather,* arrived at an unsurpassable apogee with Quentin Tarantino's *Pulp Fiction* and, above all, has time only for movies in colour and in English. No subtitles, please – no subtitles and no subtleties! In the past critics frequently got things wrong, but at least they were looking in the right direction. These days they are more interested in, say, Michael Curtiz or his exact contemporary equivalent, James Cameron, than in Kenji Mizoguchi or Mañoel de Oliveira. Like Saint Augustine eternally deferring his vow of chastity, one can almost hear them praying before a press show: 'Oh Lord, make this film good – but not that good.' They're as terrified of genius as a Hollywood mogul.

# 1965 Blow Up

The colours, once shiny-bright, gaudily psychedelic, have faded, have become a melancholy wash. I refer exclusively to the still's colours: those of the film, should you care to see it, are intact. But although I could have selected a more richly saturated image, I preferred after all to settle for this one. The sixties, too, of which *Blow Up* was one of the emblematic artefacts, have faded, faded to the point of absolute extinction, their fidgety dazzle and airily choreographed hubbub striking us now as vulgar and factitious. Thus, in the case of the image opposite, a purely technical and correctable degradation has also served as the allegory of an irreversible decline of fortune.

Something of the film does remain nevertheless; or somebody: its director, Michelangelo Antonioni, now neglected yet one of the masters of filmic modernity. How, though, in 1995, is it possible to revisit that modernity? Paradoxically, via Hitchcock.

In 1960 the auteurists felt vindicated. How, they thought, how could Hitchcock's status as a major filmmaker be disclaimed when he had had the audacity in *Psycho* to flout an immemorial genre convention by killing off his star, Janet Leigh, barely half-an-hour into the film's running time? And, to be sure, *Psycho,* its director's most successful feature in commercial terms, has ever since been regarded as a near-perfect distillation of his beadily entropic appraisal of humankind. There was, however, another event from 1960 that's also worth recalling, the contemptible catcalling which greeted the première screening of Antonioni's *L'Avventura* at the Cannes Festival. *L'Avventura* was an extraordinarily innovative work, too innovative for Cannes, but what particularly infuriated the *festivaliers* was that the film's ostensible protagonist, Anna (Léa Massari), abruptly disappears from a deserted island in the Lipari archipelago (in which the film's first section is set) and is never seen again.

Hitchcock and Antonioni therefore applied curiously identical strategies to their films: yet one was admired, the other vilified; Hitchcock's is one of the most enduringly conjurable names in the history of the cinema, Antonioni's less and less so. One wonders why. Beyond a universal preference for Hollywood films over all others, the answer surely lies in the concept of 'real time', in the spectator's conviction (or illusion) that time as it is being experienced on the screen is exactly coterminous with the time it takes to watch it unfold. Except for his experiments with the 'ten-minute take' in *Rope* and *Under Capricorn,* Hitchcock had recourse to real time only in brief, spasmodic fragments of his films, in their moments of intensest suspense (in *Psycho,* for example, when the detective Arbogast climbs the stairs, step by creaking step, of the Bates Motel). For Antonioni, by contrast, real time was a generator not of suspense but of

*suspension* – suspense purified, suspense left 'suspended', liberated from the conventional linearity of cause and effect, deliberately denying the spectator the generic gratification of knowing that 'something is about to happen'. Hitchcock's vision was circumscribed by the closed structures of a Hollywood genre (the thriller), whereas Antonioni was able to embrace the open-endedness of genuine modernity.

*Blow Up,* in which a modish photographer (David Hemmings) is persuaded that a murder has unwittingly swum into his camera's ken, can hence be read as a response to and critique of Hitchcock's *Rear Window,* which has another photographer (James Stewart) detecting another murder while spying on his neighbours through his telephoto lens. Both films reflect the implicit voyeurism and impotence of the spectator's own situation in the auditorium. The difference is that, while Stewart not merely records the crime but actually succeeds in apprehending the criminal, thereby satisfactorily closing off the narrative, neither Hemmings nor the spectator ever truly learns whether a murder was committed or not.

What it is, then, that lies at the narrative core of *Blow Up,* and what it is, by extension, that distinguishes Antonioni from Hitchcock and the modern from the 'pre-modern', is not so much a McGuffin as what might be termed a McGodot.

# 1966 Au hasard Balthazar

Two hands, one face down, so to speak, the other face up, not – no, not quite – touching. Around these two hands a blur: the natural serration of wood (the felled trunk of a tree?); a striped, buttoned fabric (a shirt?); a pullover's cuff. Robert Bresson, unquestionably. *Au hasard Balthazar*.

Before becoming a filmmaker – or rather, a cinematographer, as he preferred to define himself – Bresson had been a painter. 'Painting,' he once wrote, 'taught me to make not beautiful images but *necessary* ones.' What was implied by such a manifesto was, of course, that a too consciously assumed ambition on the artist's part to apprehend 'beauty', beauty as a value in and of itself, disconnected not only from meaning but from all the divers narrative, stylistic and formal parameters by which a work of art is articulated, cannot result in anything but empty, non-functional prettification.

For a motivated spectator Bresson's films are in fact among the most beautiful in the entire history of the cinema, but it would be hard to extract from any of them what is conventionally regarded as a beautiful shot, with the faint hint of the postcard that such a phrase inevitably conveys. The individual shot, for Bresson, represented not a cynosure but a decoy, not a spectacle but a unit. 'Film can be a true art,' he again declared, 'because in it the author takes fragments of reality and rearranges them in such a way that their juxtaposition transforms them.' And 'Each shot is like a word, meaning nothing by itself . . . it is lent meaning by its context.'

As was the case with some of the century's greatest artists (but with a mere handful of filmmakers), Bresson regarded creation as a process, primarily, of excision, ellipsis and elimination, of paring, cropping and cutting away. If his work could be characterized by a single rhetorical trope, that trope would be synecdoche. What is the point of complacently showing everything? he would argue. What is the point of showing the whole when the part can invest the same image, metonymically, with an even intenser mystery and rigour? Hence, no doubt, the extraordinary number of shots in his films, inexplicably resonant shots at that, of *parts of things* – a wheel instead of an automobile, a doorknob instead of an apartment, two not quite touching hands instead of . . . what? (As Bresson's *mise-en-scène* proceeds to cast its mesmerizing spell, the wider context gradually ceases to apply its habitual pressure and the part ends by usurping the part, or role, usually assigned to the whole.) Hence, too, the extreme importance in these films of offscreen space, with many of their most vital turns of event unfolding just beyond the frame of the screen. In Bresson's conception of cinema the act of editing implied not merely cutting between shots but also cutting *within* them, 'editing', or dissecting, those elements of which they were

composed, bodies, objects, buildings, whatever.

Bresson the minimalist? Hardly. For if 'minimalism' is a handy enough critical commonplace for describing any such radical attitude to filmic representation, it cannot do justice to the *invention* with which, from film to film, he would communicate the fundamental meaning of a scene through a flurry of guillotine-sharp images so incisively edited together they seemed to vibrate like sounds – to *whir*.

A word, finally, about Bresson and actors, appropriately enough with a film like *Au hasard Balthazar,* whose protagonist is a donkey. It is, effectively, the performances in his films that are most often accused of alienating audiences. Yet, expressionless and even zombielike as his (invariably non-professional) performers may strike the casual eye, it's an easily verifiable fact that, as with utterly conventional filmmakers, there are great Bresson performances, there are good ones and there are a few relatively poor ones. Balthazar? It gives one of the great performances; and its death, as it expires among a flock of grazing sheep to the not at all incongruous accompaniment of Monteverdi, is one of the cinema's most moving.

# 1967 Playtime

It may well be that the highlight of any communal excursion to the cinema is less some specific scene from the movie itself than that glowing aftermath of shared recollection (in the foyer, in the street, in a restaurant) during which we find ourselves, maybe only minutes from its closing credits, *already* reminiscing about it. It's during such a conversation, too, that some of us still have recourse to a type of enthusiasm that would provoke an indulgent smile if an infant were to have expressed it. 'Do you remember the scene where . . .?' we burble excitedly. Or even 'Did you see the scene where . . .?' *Do you remember?* – as if, only ten minutes after the film had ended, we were likely to have forgotten it! *Did you see?* – as if, inside the cinema, we might have fallen asleep or suddenly gone blind! Only the irrationality of certain basic forms and norms of human communication – as when, for example, with illogical indiscrimination, we call out 'Is that you?' down a darkened stairwell – can explain and excuse such childishness.

Except, though, in so far as Jacques Tati's *Playtime* is concerned. For the spectator of *Playtime* the answer to neither of the above questions is a foregone conclusion. So generously stocked with gags is the film, one might well have missed more than the odd one; and so democratic, so dialectical, is the disposition of these gags across the vast expanse of the screen (almost never in close-up, seldom foregrounded, often tucked away in a corner virtually out of sight) that it's rigorously impossible to respond to all of them on a single viewing. In *Playtime* the screen is a playground, and the critic Jonathan Rosenbaum rightly remarked that it's the only film in the history of the medium which not only has to be seen several times but each time from a different seat and section in the auditorium, the spectator thereby becoming a surrogate director, selecting and reselecting his own angles of vision from screening to screening. As Tati himself, in the guise of the gentle, lopsided Hulot, wanders through the mammoth glass-and-steel metropolis constructed specially for the film, we come to understand that the city which *Playtime* conjures up for us represents a precocious form of virtual reality.

Fittingly enough, the correct word for the film's complex spatio-temporal organization is not 'structure' but 'architecture'. *Playtime* is not only set in a city, it *is* a city. One can, as I say, lose one's way in it, one sightsees very selectively, one can never hope to understand its complete topography. But then, nothing is as like a city as the cinema. Each is a multifarious mesh of signs and an open-ended proliferation of perspectives; a semiotic Utopia; an organically self-containing, self-germinating construct, interior and exterior, private and public, pre-programmed and random. Each of them, no less, is a potentially

inexhaustible anthology of stories.

The city and the cinema. Just as there exist impersonal, characterless movies, so there exist impersonal, characterless cities – notably, those slung-together jumbles of filling stations, fast food outlets and motel bungalow courts which punctuate the American hinterland and resemble each other as much as most average American movies resemble each other. By contrast, there are also what might be called, after *films d'auteur,* instantly identifiable *villes d'auteur* (Paris, Venice, New York), each of them with its own stylistic trademark (the Eiffel Tower, the canals, the skyscrapers), just as have the classic films of Clair, Visconti and Woody Allen.

The most extreme, and perhaps most haunting, cases of all have been the cinema's *imaginary* cities, those follies erected exclusively for use in a single film, vertiginously telescoping the above analogy until, as with *Playtime,* city and film coincide absolutely. Of these, Tati's apart, one might cite Lang's *Metropolis*; Murnau's *Sunrise*; the dreamy, studio-recreated Las Vegas of Francis Ford Coppola's *One From the Heart*; and, finally, the twenty-first-century Los Angeles of Ridley Scott's *Blade Runner*, a steamy, overpopulated, neon-lit monstrosity, a city as beautiful and original as any in Italo Calvino's novel *Invisible Cities* and without question the most convincing futuristic megalopolis the cinema has ever given us.

# 1968 2001: A Space Odyssey

If Stanley Kubrick's *2001: A Space Odyssey* is wanting in anything, it is, paradoxically, in a sense of space. A sense, to be more exact, of that which used naïvely to be referred to as 'outer space'. *2001* is, by a collateral paradox, memorable above all as a film of *interiors* – like the interior, precisely, illustrated on the opposite page. The dislocation of spatial parameters inside the film's various spacecraft; the M. C. Escher-like illogicalities by which convexity metamorphoses into concavity, projection into recession and inside into outside; the space hostess (as one says 'air hostess') who, if she wants to enter the passenger cabin, must perform a three-hundred-and-sixty-degree turn, as if caught in a vertically revolving door; the ball-point pen which floats out of one passenger's pocket to the accompaniment of the 'Blue Danube' waltz; the astronauts jogging placidly around a cosmic treadmill: it's to these modestly contained conceits that the incontrovertible magic of Kubrick's film can be traced.

It is, on the other hand, in the numerous scenes set supposedly deep in external space, in Space itself, that the near-abstract co-ordinates of cosmic infinity are inadequately simulated by the depthless, two-dimensional illusionism of a gigantic backdrop, of the vastest expanse of *trompe-l'oeil* imaginable. In actual fact, this illusionism impresses the spectator as neither totally two-dimensional nor totally three-dimensional in effect (it certainly never convinces us that the 'space' it delineates could be *penetrated* by the spacecraft which drift so elegantly in the foreground) but, instead, as a weird combination of both. Here as elsewhere, Kubrick, admired as a visionary, as a mad Hegelian dreamer, demonstrates that he is instead the cinema's supreme tautologist. Space is space, his film informs us. Resembling nothing but itself, it squats on the screen, flat, matte, even klunky, without shadow zones either literal or figurative, a manifestation of million-dollar literalism rather than an authentic vision.

Tribute must nevertheless be paid to the indelibility of much of *2001*'s imagery, in particular to the creation of HAL, the overreaching computer, singing 'Daisy, Daisy' while his plugs are pulled one by one, and to the film's incalculable influence on all subsequent science-fiction in the American cinema. This direct influence is perceptible in literally hundreds of Hollywood movies, from the mystico-theological underpinning of Spielberg's *Close Encounters of the Third Kind* to the neo-medieval reverie of John Badham's *War Games,* in which the vertiginous technology of artificial intelligence is mythologized as a modern equivalent of the Philosopher's Stone (with John Wood as a Merlin-like sorcerer and Matthew Broderick as, naturally, the sorcerer's apprentice, cute and uncannily Mickey Mousish). It is, in fact, quite impossible to imagine the

cinema of the seventies and eighties, when space became a familiar, almost
humdrum, location, without Kubrick's prior example.

I recall how, visiting acquaintances in Paris during the early eighties, I fell into
conversation with their son, an intelligent child of seven-and-a-half, about the
then current films he had most enjoyed. The titles he cited were, in the main,
dishearteningly predictable ones: not *2001*, as it happens, but the films which it
influenced, the *Star War* chronicles, *Battlestar Galactica* and so on. Urged by me
to broaden – or maybe, adopting a cosmological point of view, to curb – his
cinematic horizons, he mentioned at last a film which had (to my mind,
inexplicably) done sellout business in the city, Jamie Uys' South African farce of
Coca-colonization, *The Gods Must Be Crazy*.

'And where does that film take place?' I enquired, all innocence.

Came the mildly terrifying reply: 'On earth.'

# 1969 Sayat Nova

## *The Colour of Pomegranates*

If ever film were poem, it is Sergei Paradzhanov's *Sayat Nova* (or *Nran Gouyne*), which is to a run-of-the-mill movie what an illuminated manuscript is to a paperback reprint. Barthes, in *S/Z*, coined an ingenious term for those devices of suspense and postponement by which an author (or rather, the text itself) holds the reader in seductive, Scheherazadesque thrall: he called them a narrative's 'sense of preservation'. Following Barthes, I'm tempted to call the narrative of *Sayat Nova* literally *suicidal*. As a suite of tableaux from the life of the Armenian poet Arutiun Sayadian, it has, as a strictly filmic entity, 'nowhere to go'. It lacks, in short, a point of gravity, and it's that same gravity which is absent from many of its component shots (as from the image opposite), icons of an incomparably ethereal grace, in which individual figures, whether singing, dancing, swaying or gazing serenely into the camera lens, are very seldom positioned on the 'ground floor', as it were, of the shot, but perch upon ladders, rooftops and so on.

Nor do any of these shots succeed their immediate forerunners in obeisant accordance with the precepts of classical or contemporary montage. They are, instead, laid out before our eyes like so many Tarot cards, in such an apparently disordered fashion that, were it not for the biographical continuity articulating the film, they could conceivably be reshuffled and redealt at random to engender a different but no less viable fiction (as with the Tarot-inspired tales of Calvino's *The Castle of Crossed Destinies*). Or else, to switch metaphors (and, considering the extreme hermeticism of its cluster of sociohistorical referents, the film may most fruitfully be approached by a Western spectator as a marvellous *machine à métaphores*), its images appear to be suspended in time, *hung* on the screen as in a gallery, their relation to one another contiguous, not continuous. Our scrutiny of them is utterly 'free', vertiginously 'open'; consequently, in spite of its wilful archaism, as equally its almost grating visual beauty, *Sayat Nova* may be redefined as a crucial *video* text.

What it does, too, is retrieve one of the medium's immemorial, now all but lost, vocations, the naming, through images, of objects. A pomegranate in Paradzhanov's hands, to take only the most obvious example, is transmuted into the very quintessence of what might be called 'pomegranatude' (a transmutation that cannot, for us, exclude the fruit's decadent, nineties, Wildean connotations). It has, in addition, by some mysterious alchemical process, been elevated to upper-case status, *capitalized,* so that, in even so realistic a form as the cinema, it contrives to retain the hallucinatory force of the Loaf of Bread and Jug of Wine in the *Rubáiyát,* the poem that, for a Westerner, *Sayat Nova* most

resembles. Thus it is as if pomegranates had never before been seen on the screen, or veils, masks, vases, tombstones, mandolins, statues, icons, bells, antlers, crucifixes, books, manuscripts, saddles, scales, scrolls, nipples, grapes, apples, gloves, looms, rams, loaves, lutes, daggers, towers, churches and others too luminous and numinous and numerous to list. The film's performers, too, their systematically frontal relationship to the camera already in radical defiance of the codified conventions of cinematic narrative, are framed by the director not as 'objects' for our passive gratification but rather as sacrificial victims offered up to the camera-god. There is, indeed, only one other filmmaker who has so utterly eradicated the patina of habit and familiarity with which either a performer or a filmed artefact is encrusted by the spectator's jaded eye, and that is Cocteau. His trilogy of *Le Sang d'un poète*, *Orphée* and *Le Testament d'Orphée* strikes me as far the most relevant reference where Paradzhanov is concerned.

Like the handful of other films made by this director, *Shadows of Our Forgotten Ancestors*, *The Legend of the Suram Fortress* and *Ashik Kerib*, *Sayat Nova* is a work apart, an unidentified (or, more accurately, unidentifiable) filmic object. But although, in both style and content, it gives us the impression, somehow, of *predating* the invention of the cinema, no historian of the medium who ignores it can ever be taken entirely seriously. It's a diamond of a film – but a diamond *on fire*.

# 1970  I Clowns
## *The Clowns*

In 1971 the veteran American filmmaker Frank Capra published his autobiography and called it *The Name Above the Title*. Although such a phrase may appear unbecomingly immodest, it was in fact historically justified as a reflection of the fact that, in the early thirties, when he was gradually consolidating his reputation, Capra was virtually the sole Hollywood director whose name was perceived, by both critics and public alike, as an asset, almost as a production value. It was a name, therefore, which wholly merited its unique prominence on the billing of his films.

What a long time ago that was! These days every filmmaker of note (or, frequently, of mere pretension to note) will ensure, contractually if need be, that his name is emblazoned above the title, and it's a measure of the exceptional prestige long enjoyed by Federico Fellini that his name often *was* the title. *Fellini Satyricon, Fellini Roma, Fellini's Casanova, Fellini's Interview* – rarely, in the history of a medium reputed to be of collective, collaborative inspiration, has a series of films been so intimately, exclusively, identified with the man who directed them.

But then, as I already remarked of the Cocteau of *Le Testament d'Orphée,* it's rare, too, for one to have had, when entering a cinema, so powerful an impression of also entering an artist's head. So much so, indeed, that, for any spectator who was unwilling to embark on Fellini's gaudy treadmill of circuses and comic strips, cardinals and carnivals, Barnum and ballet, there was (as, again, with Cocteau) nothing in his work, not a scene, barely even a shot, to which he could respond. Fellini was Fellini: his films were tautologies of genius.

*The Clowns.* Fellini's work may be said to distil the very *essence* of cinematic spectacle. And, critical cliché it may be, it's become impossible to refer to that work without simultaneously referring to its ultimate source of inspiration, the circus, not only as an example of pure spectacle but as one of the last genuinely communal experiences. Part of what makes his films so pleasurable is our vivid sense, simply by watching them, of what it must have been like to be involved in their creation. We actually feel transported to the vast, draught-haunted sound stages of Cinecittà, with actors, extras, freaks, sycophants and hangers-on, the by now familiar fauna and flora of Felliniana, appearing to enjoy absolutely equal status with one another; with the relaxed and negligent, sometimes infelicitous but always festive and carnivalesque *mise-en-scène* of the completed work tendering us what we cannot help suspecting is a transparent mirror image of the noisy, fractious, exuberant caravanserai that was the shoot that both

preceded and engendered it; with, above all, the cast's and crew's unanimistic faith (in the film's future, in the virtues of collective achievement, in the Maestro's own genially tyrannical presence) exuding from every pore of the screen.

*The Clowns* is, in fact, one of his later, post-*La Dolce Vita* films which dispensed altogether with narrative coherence of any conventional kind and chose instead to let fact and fantasy spin indiscriminately through the blender of his brain. It's these works which have always divided critics; as far as certain commentators are concerned, the word 'self-indulgent' might have been coined expressly for them. Fellini's own conviction, however, voiced on several occasions, was that to confine one's admiration to his early and more modestly linear films was an example of 'arrested development' and history will surely prove him right. For only a pinchpenny soul would denigrate the generosity, even on occasion the profligacy, of the powers of invention which, again and again, he displays in them. He was one of the century's great inventors of forms, and he had more ideas than he knew what to do with. If uneven, his achievement was also priceless – a curate's egg, perhaps, but by Fabergé.

# 1971  Morte a Venezia

## *Death in Venice*

Among the several problems posed by any cinematic adaptation of *Death in Venice* is that which, in relation to the character of Tadzio, might be called the Saint-Sulpician fallacy.

In theory, Mann's novella, widely regarded as the *Tristan and Isolde* of the homosexual condition (by homosexuals, that is), is as filmable as any other literary text. The fact remains, though, that Tadzio's essence as an exemplar of human beauty – beauty unjust, unearned and unwitting, by contrast with the marmoreal literary beauty laboured over by the self-consciously Goethean Aschenbach – precedes an existence founded, in the text, on a sketchy and not all that convincing verbal description. Tadzio is a Platonic ideal of male physical beauty, whose inherent transience and vulnerability Mann no less morbidly romanticizes than his youthful perfection. But how do you film an ideal? Is the artist who embarks upon such a quixotic venture not bound to commit the kind of representational solecism that (even if *Death in Venice* may appear a unique and specialized case) bedevils almost all classic literary adaptations in the cinema: fleshing out what was only a word-cluster on the page? Or, in the specific instance of *Death in Venice,* casting a 'beautiful boy' as Beauty itself?

The problem is exactly analogous to that facing any director filming the life of Christ: what to do about the codified Christ-face? If he respects it (as did Ray in *King of Kings* and Pasolini in *Il Vangelo Secondo Matteo*), then he falls into the trap of the Saint-Sulpician fallacy that I refer to above, 'Saint-Sulpician' being the term used to define the populist, arch-traditional Catholic iconography of bleeding-heart Jesuses and passive porcelain Virgins. If he rejects it (as did Scorsese in *The Last Temptation of Christ*), then he runs the risk of mythological hybridization. So too with a myth like *Death in Venice* – except that, there, the Tadzio-face, so to speak, is a strictly literary conceit, a Rorschach blot that each individual reader is free to interpret as he pleases.

Luchino Visconti's adaptation was a film of successes and failures. But while it's easy to locate the failures, no one, I feel, has sufficiently honoured the *intelligence,* a quality for which his work has rarely been admired, with which Visconti contrived the successes. For what he primarily understood was that it wasn't enough to pose his 'beautiful boy' (and the fourteen-year-old Bjørn Andresen was indeed a beauty) within the camera's field of vision and leave it at that. Thus he set up a constant, oscillating tension between the physical and the ideal, between the existence and the essence. Consider, for example, the following extraordinary passage from the film, just one of many. Watched by the

benignly smiling Aschenbach, a muddy, dishevelled Tadzio races out of the sea and is swaddled by his nurse in a robe of white towel fabric (this section filmed with a surprising, almost hand-held laxness of composition). Then, seated in a deck chair, he tosses an apple in his two hands (the frame ever so insidiously tightening its grip on the visual material). Then, to the soundtrack accompaniment of Mahler, Visconti cuts to a shot of the febrile Aschenbach, as if abruptly possessed of the demon of creation, struggling to extricate a thick bundle of papers from his briefcase. Then, if hardly more material than a shadow, a youthful silhouette flits briefly across the screen in front of him. Then, finally, the apotheosis: an exquisitely composed shot of Tadzio framed against the horizon. By virtue of the beauty of Visconti's *mise-en-scène* as much as by that of Andresen himself, Tadzio has turned into Garbo, the ideal has replaced the physical, the essence has usurped the existence.

Beyond the nostalgic homophilia, beyond the demure yet come-hither bathing costumes, beyond the Grand Hôtel des Bains, beyond Mahler's Adagio (coincidentally, when Aschenbach first notices Tadzio being summoned by his youthful companions on the beach, what he actually hears, according to Mann, is 'Adgio! Adgio!'), beyond everything, in short, that has made generations of spectators, as Truffaut once wrote, 'like the film the way they like a record and go and see it again and again', that is why I include it in this book.

# 1972 Last Tango in Paris

The title *Last Tango in Paris* has entered the language. Yet it's strangely easy to forget what an impact was made in its own day – that day being now more than twenty years ago – by Bernardo Bertolucci's story of two people who conduct an anonymous affair in a vacant Parisian flat. Easy to forget the impact of Maria Schneider's sumptuously Rubensian nakedness, of Marlon Brando's galumphing *monstre sacré* allure (the world's most famous actor playing a man who embarks on a sexual adventure on condition that his partner never ask him his name – today the part would be given, *automatically,* to Gérard Depardieu), of the once notorious 'butter scene'. Easy to forget, too – now that Vittorio Storaro, the film's cinematographer, has patented that lovely, burnished 'look' of his which, as if possessed of its own Midas touch, turns everything it caresses to gold – that there was once an authentically expressive rather than merely decorative quality to his work, a quality that could, for example, pick up on the plush and peachy tonality of Schneider's flesh tints and *douse* a whole film in them. And easiest of all to forget just how important Bertolucci seemed back in the seventies, now that he has become a fabricator of glamorous travelogues with detachable plots – *The Last Emperor, The Sheltering Sky* and *Little Buddha,* his self-styled 'exotic trilogy'. (But what neo-colonial condescension there is in that word 'exotic'!) These latter movies of his must have been fun to make, more fun, certainly, to make than to see; but then, when an artist 'sells out', it's invariably he rather than his audience that gets the best of the bargain.

Yes, it's easy to forget the impact it once made. And, in truth, it's the common fate of sexually audacious films to be overtaken, to appear unbelievably bland by subsequent standards. Who, now, would think to take exception to Gustav Machaty's *Ecstase,* with its ravishingly nude Hedy Lamarr? Or to a hitch-hiking Claudette Colbert lifting her skirt up to her knees in Capra's *It Happened One Night*? Or to the phrase 'a professional virgin' in Preminger's *The Moon is Blue*? Or, in *Sebastiane,* to Derek Jarman's naked centurions mouthing sweet gay nothings to one another, in Latin even? Or, in Polanski's *Bitter Moon,* to the verbal description by Peter Coyote of a 'golden shower' so comically ecstatic it risked provoking a wave of golden showers in the auditorium, with spectators wetting themselves in hilarity? And the question we have to ask ourselves is this: that if, from the fifties to the nineties, we have progressed from the 'professional virgin' of Preminger's *Moon* to the 'golden shower' of Polanski's *Moon,* what on earth will our children be able to see on a cinema screen in the teens and twenties of the new century? Whatever it is, it, too, one may be sure, will all too swiftly be rendered *passé* in its turn.

Yet filmmakers will, and must, continue to address the theme. I would even go

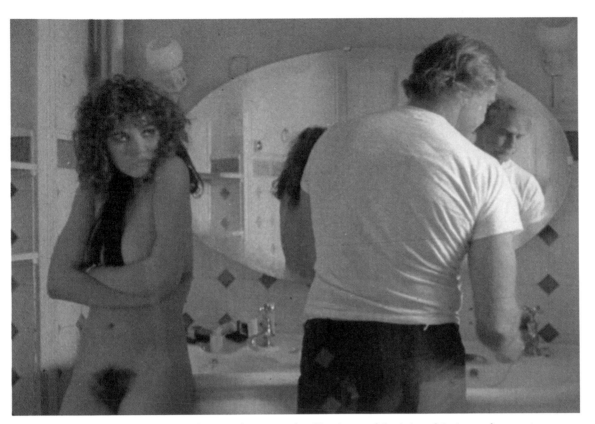

so far as to argue that a filmmaker's inherent gift of loving, of desiring, his (or, of course, her) performers constitutes, however partially and unscientifically, the one infallible measure of his contribution to the medium. For whether the object of the camera's desire be male or female, be it a 'bourgeois' body (any of the young performers of Bresson's *Le Diable probablement,* a film Truffaut thought 'voluptuous') or a proletarian one (the casts of Ken Loach's films), whether 'realistically' filmed (Sandrine Bonnaire in Agnès Varda's *Sans toit ni loi*) or mythologized (as in Coppola's *The Outsiders* and *Rumble Fish*), whether a beautiful woman (Dominique Sanda in Bertolucci's *The Conformist* and *1900*) or a beautiful boy (Matthew Barry in the same director's *La Luna*), or else representing every imaginable age, gender and social category at once (the entire cast of Rohmer's *Pauline à la plage*), the cinema is an intrinsically bisexual and even polysexual form and its motto should be that attributed to the flamboyant turn-of-the-century romancer Pierre Loti, of whom it was said that 'he loved both sexes equally; and had there been a third sex, he would have loved that as well'.

# 1973 Viskningar och Rop
## *Cries and Whispers*

In professional parlance they are called 'sleepers'. I mean those movies like, latterly, *Home Alone* and *Cyrano de Bergerac* and *The Crying Game* and *Four Weddings and a Funeral* that appear to have come out of nowhere and to general astonishment (not excluding their own makers') surpass by an extremely long way all the reasonable expectations of commercial success that were invested in them. For the non-specialist the term 'sleeper' may sound like a curious misnomer, but the intention is probably to suggest that, prior to its release, unsuspected potential slumbers deep inside certain movies and has to be awakened, like the Sleeping Beauty, by a Prince's kiss – the Prince in this instance being the public.

Movie producers are on absolutely constant alert for these sleepers; as soon as they realize that they might have one on their hands, they get behind it with a massive promotional campaign. The problem is that they haven't the faintest notion how to generate them consciously. As the screenwriter William Goldman once commented of Hollywood's ostensibly Byzantine thought-processes: *Nobody knows anything.* A sleeper, in short, fills a space which has been left vacant, except that, by definition, no one can ever know in advance that it *is* vacant or even that the space exists at all.

Ingmar Bergman's *Cries and Whispers,* his thirty-fifth film, proved to be just such a sleeper. Why so? Why, after so many films of an ineradicable pessimism (I recall a cartoon by Sempé in which a man, a Woody Allen lookalike, queueing outside a cinema in which one of Bergman's films is being screened and observing a suicidally depressed public emerge from the previous performance, turns to his companion and murmurs enthusiastically, 'Looks good!'), why, after such films as *The Seventh Seal* and *Wild Strawberries, Through a Glass Darkly* and *Winter Light, Persona* and *The Hour of the Wolf,* was he suddenly to enjoy the wide popular success that had ever eluded him in the past – with a film, to boot, whose central character (played by Harriet Andersson) is slowly, agonizingly, dying of cancer? In the preface to *Les Films de ma vie,* a published collection of his reviews, Truffaut proposed an interesting and, I believe, conclusive argument for its worldwide triumph. In the case of *Cries and Whispers,* he wrote, 'it strikes me that the film's formal perfection, and especially the use of the colour red in the décor of the house, constituted the exalting element, the element of pleasure, by virtue of which the public immediately realized that it was watching a masterpiece'. And he added – of earlier, no less beautiful works by Bergman but ones which had known only a confidential,

'happy few' sort of success – 'maybe all they lacked was red walls'.

That, it seems to me, is one of those great, simple truths which need to be aired from time to time and the airing of which is, or should be, the primary *raison d'être* of every critic. The red walls of the house in which *Cries and Whispers* is set may of course be interpreted as of a primarily symbolic nature (the red of menstruation, of blood, of death); they may equally be regarded as one of its director's most conspicuous 'signature effects' (a celebrated stage production of his, of *Hedda Gabler,* was also encased within claustrophobically red walls). Red, nevertheless, is red. Everyone likes red. Bright, sensual and primary, it's a colour to which, it's safe to assume, every normally constituted human being responds on an instinctual level. And if, notwithstanding appearances to the contrary, the contemporary cinema is inherently less pessimistic than that of the fifties, forties and thirties, it may be for no more elevated reason than that it's a cinema, almost exclusively, of colour, a cinema of *red,* a cinema in which even so allegedly grim and misanthropic a filmmaker as Bergman (such, at least, is his current reputation) is capable of charming the world merely by electing to make a film in colour, a film in red – by consenting, in short, to meet our eyes halfway.

# 1974 Céline et Julie vont en bateau
## *Céline and Julie Go Boating*

I think it fair to say that the European art film is widely regarded, even by those most respectful of its contribution to the cinema, as being no laughing matter. Yet, unexpectedly, it's a lot trickier than one might imagine to assemble a list of European art filmmakers the notion of whose filming a comedy is not simply unlikely but mind-boggling. Such a list, after all, could not include Bergman, who, albeit not latterly, was responsible for several enchanting comedies (*A Lesson in Love, Smiles of a Summer Night, Now About These Women*). Nor would it include Buñuel, nor Fellini, nor Pasolini, nor Rohmer, nor Resnais, nor Visconti, nor Duras, nor Chabrol, nor Skolimowski, in each of whose filmographies can be found at least one work designed to make us laugh, and sometimes succeeding. By contrast, the mind truly does boggle at the prospect of being tickled by a Bresson film, or one by Antonioni, Tarkovski, Straub, Angelopoulos, Pialat, Syberberg or the lugubrious Wenders. To which list of names one might have been tempted to add that of Jacques Rivette, austere, Artaudesque Rivette – were it not for *Céline et Julie vont en bateau,* the most entrancing comedy-of-manners the cinema has produced in the last thirty years.

As one would expect, however, 'comedy' is putting it a trifle too crudely. *Céline and Julie* – about the two young women of the title who, by sucking on a mysterious sweet, contrive to gain regular access (don't ask how) to a strange, spectral house and to the lives led by its stranger and even more spectral occupants – is somehow an *amused,* rather than literally amusing, film, a fiction articulated by an undercurrent of self-deflating laughter. To make sense of its narrative – partially improvised, like almost all of Rivette's work (he was a great admirer of Cassavetes) – the spectator must also be prepared to improvise, to revise his expectations from scene to scene. For the events of the film do not simply proceed from left to right, as it were, in front of one's eyes. Instead, each scene *generates* that which follows it – exactly as, in *Alice's Adventures in Wonderland* (another influence on Rivette), when Alice cries, her tears form a pool, the animals from the pool organize a race to get dry, and so forth – so that the continuity of the fictional 'procession' of events appears to advance straight ahead of one, deeper and deeper into the screen, as down a rabbit hole, forcing one to chase after it.

*Céline and Julie* might be described as a kind of filmic Tangram, that Chinese wooden puzzle out of whose seven basic components – five triangles of varying sizes, a square and a parallelogram (corresponding here, perhaps, to the house, the trio of 'ghosts' who glide through its elegant rooms, the piece of candy, and

Céline and Julie themselves) – an amazing number and variety of shapes can be fashioned. It was, for Rivette, a critical and commercial success, and its importance, as distinct from its instantly evident quality, resides precisely in that success. For it demonstrated once and for all that a theoretical, richly allusive film (with allusions to Cocteau, Minnelli, Véra Chytilová's *Daisies*) need not, by definition, be glum and po-faced. It demonstrated, equally, that the *fantastique* need not, by definition, be encumbered with a barrage of special effects (Rivette invented, for the cinema, the concept of the *light fantastic*). It demonstrated, finally, that the public (of the seventies, but now, twenty years on?) was willing to pursue a film as keenly as Céline and Julie pursue the alternative existence, the virtual reality, being lived inside what Jonathan Rosenbaum called 'the house of fiction'. And when that public emerged from the cinema, it, too, was left with a strange sweet taste in the mouth.

# 1975 Salò o le Centoventi Giornate di Sodoma

## *Salò or the 120 Days of Sodom*

It was Pier Paolo Pasolini's peculiar vocation, as a Marxist maverick, dandy (in the Baudelairean sense), poet, polemicist, filmmaker and of course homosexual, to have stirred up ideological complacencies of whatever order and rehabilitated, in the context of progressive bourgeois democracies, the old ideal of an artistic *scandal* – scandal, that's to say, as a secular blasphemy. PPP (as he became familiarly known) personified the artist as Calchas, an enemy in the Greek and Trojan camps alike, as distrusted by the mainstream Left as he was abominated by the Right. Non-partisanship, after all, is the essence of scandal, and he was nothing if not non-partisan. The Vatican that had actually awarded him a prize for his *Il Vangelo Secondo Matteo* would subsequently fulminate against the insinuations of Christian iconography in *Teorema;* whereas, in more subtle France, those intellectuals who had supported him through thick and thin, as they say, were to denounce his last and most infamous film, *Salò* (an adaptation of *Les 120 Jours de Sodome* updated to the Fascist era), as an abject betrayal of Sade's anarchic spirit.

What is *Salò?* Visually, it consists of a series of orgies, ritualized tableaux framed by the décor of the villa in which they take place. The use, however, to which Pasolini puts some of the recent past's most seductively evocative textures (Bauhaus furniture, paintings by Léger and Feininger, dance-band music and Ezra Pound on the radio) bears scant relation to the decorative, thirties-as-wallpaper aesthetic of, say, Bertolucci's *Il Conformista*. It's impossible, here, to indulge in selective nostalgia. By posing a naked girl swallowing her tormentor's warm excrement in front of the Léger, Pasolini in no sense 'romanticizes' the atrocity: rather he *defaces* the mural, as violently as, for its time, Duchamp's painted moustache defaced the Mona Lisa. He subverts an artwork that was once itself scandalous before becoming respectable museum fodder. And even had it not been justified by Sade's own fantasies, *only* excrement could have served this purpose, being the original referent of that metaphorical transference that produces graffiti, slogans painted on walls, etc.

For *Salò*, the most convincing representation of physical cruelty in film history (more than Greenaway, than Tarantino), was also one of the least metaphorical of films. Pasolini enclosed himself and his crew for fifty-two days in an isolated villa with twenty beautiful young men and women, on whom he inflicted humiliations less awful, certainly, than those depicted in the film (the excrement

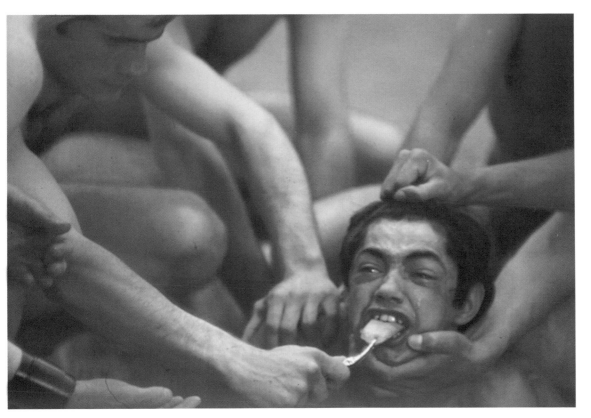

was a compound of chocolate and dry biscuit) but humiliations nevertheless.
What sort of casting sessions were held? Were sexual organs measured? Was
potential timidity put to the test? No doubt. As no doubt the mostly teenaged
hopefuls submitted with just that degree of resigned passivity (underlined in the
film itself by the dehumanizing effect of Italian postsynchronization) that
Hannah Arendt notoriously ascribed to the Jews of the Holocaust. In effect, *Salò*
could not but reflect the conditions of its own fabrication, which would thus
become the real Sadean text.

If Pasolini's very last film is still profoundly disturbing, it's not because of
what it shows but because of what it is.

# 1976 Im Lauf der Zeit
## *Kings of the Road*

There's probably a thesis to be written on the degree to which the formal and stylistic modernity of several major filmmakers can be traced to the interpolation, sometimes playful, often not, of a range of cinematic practices into the narrative substance of their films.

Hitchcock, for example, exploits the fact that, as we succumb to his shock effects, we are sitting in the dark among strangers. Bresson's direction of his non-professional performers is founded on a sadistic exploitation of the dramatic potentialities of *le trac,* or stage fright. Ozu's more static work is nearly alone in acknowledging that cinema viewing is a sedentary, contemplative occupation. Spielberg's favourite visual motif of a crowd of onlookers gawping heavenwards in wonderment tends to serve as a metaphor for the spectator's own posture of craning stupefaction when confronted with one of his science-fiction movies. And Wim Wenders' lengthy, hypnotic tracking shots owe much of their seduction to their capacity for evoking a metacinematic epiphany familiar to anyone who has idly gazed at a landscape as it disappears in the wake of a speeding car with rock music pounding on its radio.

For Wenders the cinema is a medium of *transport* – in both senses of the word. He delights in filming those conveyances that were invented at roughly the same time as the cinema itself, cars, trams, trains, aeroplanes – suave, streamlined vessels glissading across the middle distance of his compositions like the wispy, amoebic globules we occasionally glimpse floating about the corners of our eyes. No one has put it more unequivocally than he himself did: 'I don't ever want to make another film in which a car or a petrol station or a television set or a phone booth aren't allowed to appear.'

It might be said of Wenders, as was once said of Monet: He is only an eye, but what an eye! The contemporary cinema's poet of wanderlust, he contrives to incorporate into the very texture of the landscapes he films the yearning that most of us feel whenever we see a landscape, any landscape, on the screen. By the mid-seventies, when what was called the New German Cinema was at its apogee, with filmmakers like Volker Schlöndorff, Rainer Werner Fassbinder, Werner Herzog, Alexander Kluge and Hans-Jürgen Syberberg revitalizing a film culture that had been virtually moribund since the twenties, cannibalizing, with arch-German thoroughness, the politico-cultural myths of their native country, he was already starting to distance himself from his compatriots by looking westward for his inspiration. 'I learned my profession from American movies,' he said, ' . . . from Anthony Mann, John Ford and Howard Hawks.'

Above is a still from *Kings of the Road* – a quintessentially Wendersian still, like, oddly, almost every still from every film he ever made. Why so? I might cite the proto-Hawksian landscape; the cloud-stippled, Mannian sky; the truck stalled on the outer rim of the frame like a covered wagon in one of Ford's westerns. But there is, I submit, another and even more crucial factor. It's the fact that, although the parameter of motion, of rootless, restless wanderlust (of, in a word, 'Wenderslust'), strikes us as so fundamental to them, his films have a paradoxically more intimate kinship with the quirky, becalmed gaze of still photography. What he films, in short, and like a tourist of genius, are *moving photographs*. It's that fact that renders stills from his films so uniformly 'quintessential', and it's from that analogy that the doleful quality of his work primarily derives, for photography is a melancholy art.

Bushy-haired, soft-spoken, faintly stooped, Wenders is the ideal embodiment of the contemporary European filmmaker, his eyes permanently hooded by dark glasses, his camera no less permanently at those eyes like a spangly microphone at a pop singer's lips, a camera which he uses the way a blind man uses his white stick, to explore the contours of a world which would perhaps remain inaccessible to him without it.

# 1977 La Chambre verte

## The Green Room

Truffaut? What can one say about him that hasn't already been said? Everyone knows the story of his feckless adolescence, when, as others have run away from home to join the army, he ran away from home *to join the cinema*. Of his young manhood, when it was only by the intercession of André Bazin that he was rescued from delinquency and possibly outright criminality. Of his lengthy stint as a critic at *Cahiers du Cinéma,* in one issue of which, in a kind of St. Valentine's Day Massacre, he systematically liquidated the directors of what he termed, without a vestige of either irony or affection, *le cinéma de papa*. Of *Les 400 Coups* and *Tirez sur le pianiste* and *Jules et Jim,* a young man's films, endlessly inventive and (notwithstanding the dark patches that could not help but seep through) unquenchably high-spirited, which, arguably more so even than Godard's, were to epitomize an entire generation of filmmaking. And, finally, of the latter, unquestionably less stimulating period, which saw a progressive gravitation to the mainstream, to the centre, on occasion to what might even be called the *extreme-centre*. (It does exist.)

From this latter period, alas, too much of his output struck one as unworthy of a major director; and if his fairly precipitous decline can be attributed to any one externally verifiable factor, it would surely be to his decision, in the early sixties, to function as his own producer – a dual operation calling to mind the old legal chestnut about a defendant who ventures to defend himself having a fool for a lawyer. To no one's surprise, his films grew cautious and respectable, made in total compliance with the codes of mainstream French cinema. And yet . . . There was, even then, for an artist so disposed to ingratiating himself, a project as brave (for a producer) and as profoundly contrary (for a director) as *La Chambre verte*.

It was the sheer morbidity of *La Chambre verte* which made it appear so utterly *sui generis* (although Resnais' *L'Amour à mort* and Tavernier's *La Vie et rien d'autre* may since claim to bear a certain resemblance to it). As if to emphasize the unusually personal nature of the undertaking, Truffaut himself played the leading role, that of a necrophiliac obituary-writer on a provincial newspaper just after the Great War in which practically all of his friends had been killed, an individual more than half in love with easeful death and condemned to wander somnambulistically through a no-man's-land situated somewhere between life and afterlife. Rarely, indeed, had the imagery of a film seemed so fixated on candles, coffins, tombstones, chapels and every conceivable form of *memento mori*. Nor were these motifs ever shaped into flamboyantly

baroque configurations *à la* Gance or coolly poeticized *à la* Franju. On the contrary, just as the high-spirited visuals of his earlier work had embodied his characters' charm and vulnerability, so in *La Chambre verte* the very *deadness* of his style settled on the film like a heavy covering of crêpe. Yet it was, paradoxically, by such an absolute rejection of the romantic or surreal attributes of death in favour of its most conventionally Judeo-Christian trappings that he revitalized the Orphic theme in a manner hardly less radical than Cocteau thirty years before. *La Chambre verte* was arguably the director's finest and most original work; it was, now unarguably, one of the great films of the nineteen-seventies.

And yet again . . . Truffaut wrote somewhere that he always preferred to end his films in a burst of sunlight, as a reward to the spectator for having endured two hours of darkness. And, writing earlier on *The Cure,* I regretted the fact that he had never filmed *L'Alouette,* the play in which Anouilh contrived a happy ending to the life of Joan of Arc. So let's give his life, too, a happy ending – let's flash back to the Truffaut of the sixties, the Truffaut of the *nouvelle vague,* the youthful, fierce, incurably romantic Truffaut, *Pierrot le sage* to Godard's *Pierrot le fou,* each of whose films represented a joyous manifestation of professional and emotional camaraderie (or camera-derie).

# 1978  L'Hypothèse du tableau volé
## *The Hypothesis of the Stolen Painting*

There is, to begin with, the name. Raúl Ruiz. Or Raul Ruiz. Or Raoul Ruiz. 'Ruiz' was, of course, Picasso's middle name; and, figuratively speaking, 'Picasso' might be said to be Ruiz's middle name. Or one might relocate the name 'Ruiz' in the middle of that belonging to another insatiable storyteller: Scheheruizade. Or one might include him in the list of prolific, *torrential* artists, beside Picasso in painting, Milhaud and Villa-Lobos in music, Feuillade and Fassbinder in film. Or else, in an attempt to define his unique and startling contribution to the contemporary cinema, one might paraphrase Cocteau on Orson Welles: He (i.e. Welles or Ruiz) 'is a kind of giant with the look of a child, a tree filled with birds and shadows, a dog that has snapped its chain and lies down in the flower beds, an active idler, a wise madman, an island surrounded by people, a schoolboy asleep in class, a strategist who pretends to be drunk when he wants to be left in peace.'

Ruiz's existence seems to consist of a perpetual shoot: only God knows (for I doubt that Ruiz himself does) how many films he has made, and even God couldn't have found the time to see them all. Specialized journals have devoted entire issues to his output. Rare is the festival these days which cannot boast a new Ruiz film. There exists a Ruiz-effect, a Ruiz-system, a Ruiz-myth. As an artist, he has long since become subject to what might be defined as the Law of Expanding Returns – to the point where, were he to append his signature to a frying-pan, let's say, that signature would oblige us to revise our perception of Ruiz's career, of the cinema, of the utensil itself, and possibly of the world.

Ruiz made *L'Hypothèse du tableau volé* in 1978 after years of exile from his native Chile. It was an apolitical 'art movie' in a hallowed, if by then somewhat discredited, Parisian tradition and it was based on a contemporary literary classic, *Le Baphomet,* by the novelist and Nietzschean philosopher Pierre Klossowski. Notwithstanding such apparently unimpeachable cultural foundations, however, Ruiz, as ever, contrived to avoid ingratiating himself with his backers, the redoubtable INA. *L'Hypothèse,* as it transpired, was less a straight adaptation than a witty series of variations on Klossowskian (and Ruizian) themes. The pearly black-and-white cinematography by Sacha Vierny, a pastiche of Henri Alekan's for Cocteau's *La Belle et la Bête,* was just too grey for comfortable television viewing (INA was a commissioning body for French TV). As for his cast, their potential for histrionics was effectively neutralized by their obligation, throughout the film, to adopt and sustain a series of kitschy *tableau vivant* postures (see above) – Diana pursued by Actaeon, a game of chess

played by two Knights Templar, a naked, martyred youth with the glittering torso of an arrowless Sebastian – during which they were also supposed to *fidget,* surely the most difficult thing to request of any trained actor.

The film is a *jeu d'esprit,* but an especially refined and brilliant one, which proposes a reflection on four types of representational space – pictorial, sculptural, cinematic and, less easily describable, that curious amalgam of all three whose most innocent expression might be the diminutive, exquisitely layered vistas one peers at through a Viewmaster device. And so rarefied is the kitsch as to have become well-nigh indistinguishable from the Olympian 'high art' that it cunningly parodies. A postmodern artefact, in short.

Which is basically all I wished to say about *L'Hypothèse du tableau volé,* as about its director, still too little-known in English-speaking countries. Except that I should like to pose a naïve but, I believe, pertinent question – pertinent not merely to Ruiz but to more contemporary filmmakers than one might imagine, to Straub on occasion, Godard on frequent occasion, Tarkovski and Kieślowski sometimes. This is the question: *Is it possible to admire a film, and even consider it a masterpiece, without actually understanding it?* For no article that I have ever read (or, indeed, written) on Ruiz's films has persuaded me that the author of said article (myself not excluded) has any real idea what these films are ultimately, as they say, 'all about'.

# 1979 Apocalypse Now

A lowering helicopter, billows of black and punkishly red smoke, a group of ochre-coloured American soldiers scrambling for cover – it was this imagery, the imagery, most memorably, of Francis Ford Coppola's *Apocalypse Now,* which ever after epitomized the filmic recreation of the Vietnam war.

It was with *Apocalypse Now,* too, that it became evident which role Vietnam war movies were playing in the contemporary American cinema: that of 'the return of the repressed'. For over a decade (in fact, for almost precisely the term of its own duration) Hollywood had conspicuously *censored* a war which had been monopolizing the various media forums for national debate, with the result that the imagery through which the public grew accustomed to the Vietnam experience was for many years exclusively televisual in origin. As was often noted, it had been a war fought without songs; for a long time it seemed fated as well to be memorialized without fictions. Yet, eventually, so many Vietnam war films were produced that they could legitimately be regarded as constituting a genre of their own. Like the two World Wars that preceded it, Vietnam gradually started to engender a self-sufficient set of generic conventions and assumptions – the assumption, for example, that it was the conflict itself rather than the near-holographic, on occasion even invisible, Vietcong which represented the true enemy; the virtual absence of the officer class and the correspondingly privileged status of the grunt's point of view; and the implication that a veteran was, almost by definition, a profoundly disturbed individual, possessed of that glassy-eyed 'thousand-yard stare' that infallibly distinguished the breed. At the same time, and mostly by virtue of Coppola's film, the war was to acquire a universally acknowledged signifier: the helicopter. Should a chopper happen to swim into the camera's field of vision, it was a foregone conclusion that, no matter where the movie's narrative was nominally set, the spectre of south-east Asia was hovering somewhere nearby.

What Hollywood for so long repressed had returned to haunt it. For there seemed, did there not, to be *something wrong* with Cimino's *The Deer Hunter* and Kazan's *The Visitors* and Stone's *Platoon* and Coppola's *Apocalypse Now,* some malaise gnawing at their innards, prompting an obscure and unavowed sense on the spectator's part that they were not as other movies were. When we emerged from a film about Vietnam, we somehow knew we wouldn't be allowed to confine our response to 'I liked it' or 'I didn't like it'. A genuinely *critical* position-taking was expected of us, one that was usually related to the film's ideological soundness or absence thereof. Likewise, Hollywood directors appeared to realize that when they made a Vietnam, or Vietnam-related, film, they were putting themselves on the line in a way that did not arise with any

other genre. And it was finally made clear that, external appearances notwithstanding, the Vietnam war movie was (or is, but it may well have run its course) a *psychological,* not an action, genre, in which the war's function was analogous to one of those perennial 'burning issues' (so beloved of the makers of high-minded television dramas) that are designed to reveal character and test the fibre of a society: racism, for example, is another, as is rape and drug addiction and, of course, Aids.

And the Vietnamese? Invisible, as I have said, as invisible from the American cinema of Vietnam as from the American soldiery in Vietnam. Yet there was a moment in one of the later Vietnam films which represented a first for the genre and may be compared, *toutes proportions gardées,* to that primal scene of American literature in which, aboard the raft of *Huckleberry Finn,* Huck forces himself to apologize for playing a callous practical joke on the black slave Jim – to apologize, in short, for the first time in his life, to a nigger. The moment arises in Oliver Stone's *Born on the 4th of July,* and it follows the 'wasting' of a Vietnamese hamlet through an avoidable confluence of circumstances. Inside one of its little straw huts the movie's protagonist (played by Tom Cruise) confronts the mangled victims of his unit's firepower. And, with tears brimming in his big blue American eyes, he utters the hackneyed phrase of penitence, easily formulated, hideously inadequate, yet sacred, too, for all that: 'Forgive me.'

# 1980  Raging Bull

Droll De Niro. For what a curious figure Robert De Niro is. The finest actor of the American cinema's post-Brando generation (Nicholson, Hoffman, Pacino, etc.), he has also, perversely, seemed determined to emulate Brando's pitiful decline into numbing repetition and outright eccentricity. So statufied, in recent years, have his patented tics become, one has sometimes had the impression of watching him give, as though on stage rather than screen, his thousandth weary performance of the same part. Indeed, one cannot help wondering whether, even in terms of its strictly physical transformation, the role he played in Martin Scorsese's *Raging Bull* (already all of fifteen years ago!) might have been a premonitory allegory of his own subsequent deterioration as a performer.

We all know what De Niro had to undergo to play that role – of the 1949 middleweight champion Jake La Motta, from cocky young contender to cocktail lounge has-been – and the still opposite is more eloquent than could be any verbal description of his extraordinary commitment to the portrayal (or rather, the personal *assumption*) of the depredations to which La Motta's ageing flesh was heir. The impact which such a metamorphosis had on the spectator was that of a living, breathing special effect. Yet, fascinating spectacle as it was in its own right, De Niro's heroic decision to permit his neat and natural wiriness to slacken into pot-bellied obesity (an effect unobtainable through conventional padding) was both the emblem and the *reductio ad absurdum* of the intensified 'realism' that has tended to distinguish the American cinema of the eighties and nineties from any and all of its previous manifestations. There is, for example, the fact that it's now almost unimaginable for any major Hollywood film to have recourse to 'stock shots' (a practice, nevertheless, long enshrined in film history); the fact that any four-letter words may be uttered and, short of unsimulated copulation, any 'four-letter acts' performed in a mainstream feature; the fact that even populist directors have ceased to balk at subtitling those passages of their movies set in a foreign country; the fact that the pastiche of newsreel footage has of late come to acquire a hallucinatory technical plausibility (*Zelig* and *Forrest Gump*); and so on.

Whatever more personal claims may be made for him, Scorsese is the absolute master of such *material* realism. So much so that he has been at constant risk of overreaching himself: filming, in *The Color of Money,* the pool table as if it were an arena of potentially explosive violence (billiard balls slamming against each other in close-up like bowling balls), whereas the spectacle of the real game of pool is primarily of a strategic and topological nature, and 'vernacularizing' the characters of *The Last Temptation of Christ,* as if being Jewish in contemporary Brooklyn were socioculturally identical to having been Jewish in the Middle East

of two millennia ago. It's ironic that Scorsese has been beatified as the greatest American filmmaker (and *Raging Bull* voted the greatest American film of the eighties) at a stage in his career when he is producing what, for the director of *New York, New York* and especially *King of Comedy* (one of the finest movies made anywhere in the last thirty years) is substandard work. Even in a relative success like *GoodFellas* one has an uneasy sense of his freewheeling on an admittedly formidable métier, indulging a weakness for hollow, drumroll pyrotechnics more typical of a Brian De Palma or an Alan Parker and displaying a predilection for the sort of over-studied effect that announces, to those unsure of the exact function of a director, that *here is a film that has been directed.* Although he has often expressed his admiration for Michael Powell, a more appropriate comparison might be made with another British director, Carol Reed, whose cod-expressionist cinematography in *Odd Man Out* was reminiscent, in advance, as it were, of Scorsese's self-conscious stylistics.

*Scorsese.* Although that name rhymes, of course, with 'Maisie', it has always made me think of words like 'journalese' and 'legalese', words denoting the petrified discourse of a language that was once fresh and challenging. Such petrifaction is now the primary danger confronting a good, but not necessarily great, filmmaker. And, from the evidence of his recent work, the omens, as with De Niro, are not favourable.

# 1981 Napoléon

If Abel Gance's *Napoléon* was obviously not made in 1981 (it dates from 1927), it was, in a sense, *remade* in 1981, by Kevin Brownlow and David Gill. For it was in that year that the film, which had been unseen for several decades in any form approximating that in which Gance intended it, was restored by Brownlow and Gill to more or less its former splendour. It was hence from that year, too, that the whole growth industry of modern cinematic restoration may be dated: at first exclusively of silent classics or near-classics (Sjöström's *The Wind,* Raoul Walsh's *The Thief of Bagdad,* Harold Lloyd's *Safety Last,* among others); then, more splashily, of a series of mainstream movies (Cukor's *A Star Is Born,* Scorsese's *New York, New York,* Kubrick's *Spartacus*) that many of us could still remember from the first time around. Preservationists, in effect, are now no longer willing to wait until some favourite movie has to be patched together from occasionally ill-fitting shreds of celluloid from the vaults of a half-dozen different film libraries. And, of course, one advantage of addressing the task years rather than decades after a film's original theatrical release is the odds-on chance of the director himself still being available to help the restorer figure out what goes where.

It's mostly thanks to Brownlow and Gill, then, that the eighties and nineties have witnessed the return of the medium's silent imagery to iconographic status in the popular imagination. Paradoxically, however, just as the silent cinema is becoming fashionable again, the films themselves have been, so to speak, de-silenced. For *Napoléon,* precisely, Carl Davis was commissioned to write a new, full-length score to accompany the film 'live' at its first screenings. (Honegger's original incidental music was seemingly just twenty minutes long.) And the pioneering triumph of Davis's romantic pasticcio has led to some rather outlandish developments – Giorgio Moroder's pseudo-postmodern revamping of *Metropolis* and a public performance of Eisenstein's *Alexander Nevsky* for which Prokofiev's superb score was detached from the film's soundtrack and duplicated live in the auditorium. (In this instance it's the 'live', not the recorded, version that deserves to be called the duplicate.)

Apparently alone, as an unreconstructed disciple of Henri Langlois, who would disallow accompanying music of any kind when he had silent films screened at the Cinémathèque Française (on the grounds that the cinema had its own rhythms, its own harmonies), I have never been, and still am not, convinced. Do Brownlow and Gill not comprehend that silence itself may function as a *score*? Does Davis not realize that sonorizing Gance's film as he has done isn't so very different from colourizing it? Cannot Moroder see that an equivalent in art history to his glitzy reprocessing of *Metropolis* for the fast-

forward generation would be the wiring up of *The Laughing Cavalier*, with great, genial haw-haws booming out from a sound-box concealed behind the canvas? There's a word for this, and it's 'kitsch'.

But I seem to be concentrating on sound alone in a book that is, after all, primarily devoted to pictures. My excuse is that, in all the hoohah surrounding its orchestration, it has become bizarrely easy to forget that *Napoléon* is a work *solely* composed of images. And, oh, those images! Gance suspended his camera from a wire and strapped it on to a galloping horse and mounted it on a pendulum and just stopped short of having it zoom to the moon like a rocket. He filmed 3-D footage which, for some reason, he elected not to incorporate into the completed narrative. Most famously, of course, he split his screen three ways. Yet, brilliant as *Napoléon* is, quite breathtaking, in fact, and of undeniable importance in the history of the cinema, watching it is, as someone once said, not unlike reading a novel in which each and every sentence is punctuated by an exclamation mark. If masterpieces were a genre, *Napoléon* would be a masterpiece; but, there it is, they aren't, and it isn't.

The still which illustrates this essay is symptomatic of the film as a whole. Its sheer spectacle can scarcely be denied; nor, surely, can its (and I weigh my words) fundamental vulgarity and naïveté. It would make a marvellous jigsaw puzzle, though.

# 1982  White Dog

Everything in a film is ultimately contingent upon the extent to which it does or does not assume its own subject matter. In *White Dog* (and, when discussing it, one has to forget the made-for-TV-movie ramifications of its occasionally rather conventional plotting, as they're of strictly no importance) Samuel Fuller's subject matter is racism. A 'white dog' is one which, by being systematically abused and mistreated from puppyhood by a hired black drug addict (generally one in need of ready cash), grows up conditioned to attack members of the black race alone.

The German Shepherd of Romain Gary's original factual account served primarily as a symbol, a metaphor, a focus for the author's moist humanitarian reveries on the assassination of Martin Luther King, on the campus rioting of the late sixties, on the Black Panthers (with some of whom he was personally acquainted through his then wife, the actress Jean Seberg) and on racial tensions in general. In Fuller's cinema, however, a spade tends to be almost viscerally present as a spade. Like Dr Johnson refuting the exponents of metaphysical scepticism by treating external reality to a hefty kick in the shins, he is prepared not merely to call a spade a spade but to slam it into the public's face as an irrefutable demonstration of its physical existence. Hence, in his movie, the dog is a very real dog. No matter how the narrative spirals out to encompass the director's characteristically gutsy metaphorizing of emotion and violence – of, one might even say, emotion *as* violence – it remains a frightening, menacing, *animal* presence. And what separates *White Dog* from the conventional anti-racist homilies of such professional humanists as Stanley Kramer and the slightly more estimable Martin Ritt, and what was doubtless at the centre of the otherwise baffling protests that prevented it from enjoying a proper distribution within the United States and long delayed its European release, is that for Fuller the representation of racism, too, is above all physical in essence. With a single stroke his movie sweeps aside the whole sociopolitical *pathos* of the racial question, from the lumberingly schematic allegory of Kramer's *The Defiant Ones* (which had Tony Curtis and Sidney Poitier playing a couple of escaped convicts handcuffed to one another on whom it slowly dawns that they are in reality handcuffed by – message! message! – the chains of their common humanity) to the green pastures and purple patches of Spielberg's *The Color Purple,* from the excesses of Douglas Sirk's *Imitation of Life* to the inadequacies of Guy Green's *A Patch of Blue.*

*White Dog* is a film about racism – therefore (but that 'therefore' is probably a first for world cinema) it's a film about *skin*. Fuller's black characters are only incidentally the more or less acquiescent victims of socio-economic inequality;

they are, first and foremost, as is reflected in our still, men and women whose skins are black. And one of the contemporary cinema's most shocking, most unnerving single shots is that in the film of a patch not of blue nor of purple but of *flesh*, of an elderly trainer's fat, throbbing black belly filmed in close-up. In an age when, even now, the American film industry is seldom ready to advance beyond the crassest type of tokenism (with every other heist movie boasting its sassy black police sergeant, usually played by either Danny Glover or Wesley Snipes), that shot in itself was a breakthrough.

Subtlety, to be sure, has never been Fuller's forte. It has often been said of him that, a reporter before he became a director, he retains the newspaperman's snooping instinct for a scoop, for a banner headline. The very titles of his movies appear to scream out for the exclamation marks of tabloid sensationalism. Just listen to them: *I Shot Jesse James! Fixed Bayonets! Pick-up on South Street! Hell and High Water! Underworld USA! Shock Corridor! The Naked Kiss! Dead Pigeon on Beethoven Street!* This, though, is the source of his raw, primitive strength as a filmmaker, peculiarly so where a film about racism is concerned: that everything he films, even if it happens to be in the Technicolor of *White Dog*, he knows how to render in the starkest black-and-white.

# 1983 Querelle

References to the work of Rainer Werner Fassbinder have so consistently conveyed a creepy, 'decadent', almost Warholesque public image that one tends to forget that to have directed thirty-two films in just fifteen years can scarcely be considered the achievement of a foppish, cocaine-sniffing amateur. If ever a filmography testified to the rejection of dilettantism, it is his. Notwithstanding the connotations of cynicism and despair that soon attached to his name, Fassbinder was a true believer, with an artisanal faith in his chosen medium. Cavalierly appropriating the most over-determined forms of film history – the 'woman's picture' (*Veronika Voss*), the faithful literary adaptation (*Effi Briest*), the musical biopic (his delirious Mein Campf extravaganza, *Lili Marleen*), the urban thriller (*Die dritte Generation*), the Hawksian farce (*Satansbraten*), the social study *à la* Martin Ritt (*Faustrecht der Freiheit*) and the chamber drama *à la* Ingmar Bergman (*Die bitteren Tränen der Petra von Kant*) – he made radical movies the way Michael Curtiz and Raoul Walsh and Douglas Sirk made genre movies, as methodically and, in his own weird fashion, just as unselfconsciously.

His swan song, *Querelle* (based on the novel by Jean Genet), was not one of his better films, far from it; and this tackily orchidaceous shot of Brad Davis bathed in a tangerine glow as if not just he but the whole film were on heat, is equally far from being characteristic of his imagery. But there, that's precisely why I selected it. For there simply doesn't exist any 'characteristic' Fassbinder image. To a degree that can be claimed only of Godard (the pre-1968 Godard), of Resnais, Oshima, Powell, Oliveira, Ruiz and, from Hollywood, only Minnelli, Ray and (for his admirers) John Huston, not one of his works shares its visual tonality, its 'look', with any of the others. Each of his films seems consciously designed – in form, style, subject matter, photographic texture, even screen format – to controvert its predecessor in the canon. By the seventies, moreover, his visuals had curdled into near-abstract delirium. Carmen Miranda would have struck one as mousy and drab in the screwy Surrealist prism of *Lili Marleen*'s garish cinematography. That of *Lola* parodied not just the grisly DeLuxe Color of the fifties but, with its gangrenous mauves, DeLuxe Color already in a state of tonal deterioration. And the snowy, cocainy whites of *Veronika Voss* proved that Fassbinder, although one of the cinema's natural Fauves, could function no less brilliantly with a monochromatic palette.

He contrived, moreover, to treat an astonishing number of 'topical' issues, among which were terrorism, drug addiction, racism, transsexualism, the tabloid press and the so-called 'quiet despair' of middle-class existence. He anatomized the fat, complacent corruption of West Germany's postwar economic boom. And he portrayed his own sexuality with unmatched candour,

playing the grubby, urine-scented proletarian Fox in *Faustrecht der Freiheit* and exposing what were doubtless his own clammily intimate fantasies in *Querelle*. Can as much be said of any novelist or dramatist of the same period?

It was for his marathon poem of the First World War, *Discours du grand sommeil,* that Cocteau devised an image of which he must have been especially fond, as it reappeared regularly throughout his work: that of a dead soldier whose wristwatch survives him, tick-tick-ticking on as if in a metallic parody of the beating of a human heart. It was of that image that I thought when, in June 1982, I heard of Fassbinder's death from an overdose of drugs. But, if I thought of it, it wasn't merely because a video recorder was found to be imperturbably humming on inside his apartment when his body was discovered. In the face of such a direct corroboration, Cocteau's fanciful little conceit assumed (as he probably always meant it to do) an allegorical universality. For what else is Fassbinder's wristwatch but that exemplary body of work which has survived him? And it hasn't wound down yet.

# 1984 Zelig

I like Woody Allen. I like the Woody Allen of *Annie Hall* and *Broadway Danny Rose* and *Radio Days* and *Husbands and Wives*. No matter that he has made his fair share of mediocre films (*A Midsummer Night's Sex Comedy, Another Woman*), others that I regard as frankly bad (*September, Shadows and Fog*), still others that seem to me to have been deliriously overrated (*The Purple Rose of Cairo, Crimes and Misdemeanors*), no matter, too, that I have sometimes thought of him as having of late 'sold out' to high art the way other artists have been accused of selling out to commercialism, have thought, in other words, that his never exactly latent tendency to navel-gazing now risks becoming something of a joke in itself (perhaps, like Graham Greene, he ought to make more explicit the difference between his 'entertainments' and his higher-minded films, by naming himself in two distinct styles on their credits: 'Woody' for the former and 'Woodrow', say, for the latter) – notwithstanding all of that, I cannot help liking Woody Allen. At least before I see it, each of his films constitutes an indefinable little event in my life. It generates a *frisson* of pleasurable anticipation that even films by the (many) directors whose work I consider to be essentially more interesting cannot match. And I feel a similar *frisson* when the lights go down in the auditorium and, to the accompaniment of some luscious 'standard' by Gershwin, Kern or Cole Porter, I'm confronted with a whole new set of his typically austere, unvaryingly black-and-white credit-titles. With the sole exception of Spielberg, Allen is the only filmmaker without whose regular, indeed annual, contribution I simply cannot imagine contemporary American culture.

Here is an unusually sobersided Allen photographed in the company of Herbert Hoover and, as a newspaper caption would put it, 'a friend'. The movie is *Zelig*. Allen, its director, also cast himself as Leonard Zelig, its protagonist, a chameleonic nonentity who, by what might be called psychic mimesis, is so contaminated by the personalities of the great and the good whom he contrives to frequent (Chaplin, Hitler, Babe Ruth, Eugene O'Neill) that his own physical envelope begins to assume their most visible traits and attributes. The still in question has of course been doctored, and *Zelig* as a whole was such a perversely ingenious exploitation of special effects (special effects that had always been regarded as the exclusive preserve of mainstream Hollywood) that it tended to be coolly applauded as a mere *jeu d'esprit* when not dismissed outright. (One of the most expensive of Allen's movies, it was also one of his most expensive flops.) Yet, more than *Annie Hall*, than *Stardust Memories*, than *Husbands and Wives*, *Zelig* is a truly personal, covertly autobiographical work – precisely because its subject matter is the *absence*, the permanent vacancy, of personality.

The truth is that, as a filmmaker (if not as a performer), Woody Allen *has almost no personality of his own*. Respect him as we may for preferring pastiche (or imitation as the sincerest form of flattery) in a period when the American cinema has capitulated to the whorish charms of parody (or imitation as the basest form of derision), we ought not to elevate a pasticheur's talent into the temperament of an authentic artist. Allen is Zelig, Zelig is Allen. Brought into contact with Bergman, he turns into Bergman (*Interiors, Another Woman*); with Fellini, he turns into Fellini (*Stardust Memories, Radio Days*); with Pabst, he turns into Pabst (*Shadows and Fog*); with Hitchcock, he turns into Hitchcock (*Manhattan Murder Mystery*); and so it has always gone.

*Zelig,* however, is the exception that for once truly does prove the rule. For all that the name itself appears to invoke the Voltaire of *Zadig* (nor is the Jewish Kafka too far away), what the film ultimately resembles is one of Poe's more demented tales of physical duplication and psychological bifurcation. For, in this instance alone in his clever, derivative body of work, Allen is prepared to turn his camera inward by holding a mirror up to the already mirrory void at the core of his own sensibility. The only way, after all, to find out what a chameleon (Woody Allen) really looks like is to set it down on top of another chameleon (Leonard Zelig).

# 1985 Offret

## The Sacrifice

I am now prepared to make a haughtily categorical statement about film. To wit, that there exists such a thing as an 'essence' of great cinema; that, whatever their external differences, all great (or even very good) films are made in exactly the same way; and that one can tell whether a film is of any real and lasting value after five minutes or so. By which I mean that Hitchcock's *Psycho* has, *in essence,* more in common with Dreyer's *Vampyr* that with any of the crude slasher movies which would never have been made without its prior example. Or, indeed, that it has more in common with, shall we say, Eisenstein's *Ivan the Terrible* or Nicholas Ray's *Bigger Than Life* or Godard's *Pierrot le fou* or Bergman's *Fanny and Alexander* than with almost all of Hollywood's regular product. I am prepared equally to admit that I find it hard to articulate in what that essence consists, but I pride myself on instantly recognizing its absence, an absence usually rendered all too present by a dependence on what might be termed *shortcuts to emotion.* For, God knows, there are many such in current film grammar: time-lapse cinematography, with baroque clouds scudding across apocalyptic skies (Godfrey Reggio's *Koyaanisqatsi*); the narrative accompaniment of a complacent medley of romantic standards in lieu of a proper soundtrack score (Nora Ephron's *Sleepless in Seattle* among innumerable others); credit-title imagery of an automobile gliding along a sun-dappled freeway to the sound of its own radio ('. . . and it's looking to be another hot one today in downtown Houston . . .'); meticulously calculated long-shots making overly aesthetic play with tiny figures silhouetted against the horizon (Jane Campion's *The Piano*); and, of course, good old, trusty old, slow motion.

That is, of course, a completely subjective inventory, a bit whimsical and far from exhaustive. But what is left when it has been exhausted is not 'nothing', not any arid minimalism, but the kind of film which deploys its camera to *contemplate* the world instead of amplifying it – instead of *miking* it, as one says of rock operas. There are such films. And one of them is Andrei Tarkovsky's *The Sacrifice*.

What is most distinctive about our still from the film? I suggest this: the absence of spectacle, of *show business*. Tarkovsky himself captioned the image thus, in his book *Sculpting in Time:* ' "Little Man" waters the tree his father planted, patiently awaiting the Miracle which is no more than the truth.' Maybe so; but, since we should never feel coerced into unquestioningly endorsing a creator's interpretation of his own work, we may be allowed to reject so demagogically 'spiritual' a reading, even in the context of the film as a whole, as

the last word on the subject. For what could be more flatulently theoretical than that description? And what, by contrast, could be more limpid and serene and unrhetorical than the image which it purports to describe, one of several such in the film, the image of an infant (neither a Hollywood cutie nor a glum, unprepossessing, Bergmanesque brat) craning up at the branches of a trec (which itself is uncinematically puny) against the background of a shimmering (but not dazzlingly shimmering) lake and a skyscape of placid (un-baroque, resolutely unapocalyptic) clouds? The notion of a contemporary Hollywood filmmaker being drawn to the same story as that of *The Sacrifice* – an intellectual, convinced that a nuclear holocaust is about to destroy the planet, swears to God that he will sacrifice everything he is and has, himself, his family, even the little son we see in this still, if only it needn't be so – is unlikely but not inconceivable. He could not for an instant, however, have found a visual style so mysteriously simple and beautiful in which to relate it. The clouds would be rhetorically inflated by time-lapse cinematography, the lake would be straight out of *National Geographic* magazine, the tree a giant redwood, the infant Macauley Culkin. There is show business, and then there is cinema.

# 1986 Le Rayon vert

## *The Green Ray*

I should like to propose a theory to account for the extreme, peculiar and enduring fascination of Eric Rohmer's work.

Rohmer is, I suggest, an adroit and subtle practical joker. I suggest, as well, that there's a slightly disturbing quality to his films, to the original 'Contes moraux', the subsequent 'Comédies et proverbes' and the current 'Contes des quatre-saisons'; or, more precisely, to the nature of their reputation both inside and outside their country of origin. Certainly, his fans have never been tongue-tied when it comes to articulating their enthusiasm for his films, as witness a typical chorus of satisfied customers: 'Such a *civilized* director . . .' and 'Such *intelligent* characters . . .' and, especially, 'What a pleasure to hear such *good talk* in the cinema . . .' And critics have tended to concur, aligning him with such other virtuosos of verbal dexterity as Sacha Guitry, Marcel Pagnol and Joseph Mankiewicz, as equally with such contemporary *petits-maîtres* as James Ivory, Barry Levinson and Denys Arcand. Yet, aside from the fact that equating a film's intelligence with the intelligence of its spoken dialogue is to beg a number of crucial questions, I would suggest, finally, that Rohmer's characters are not only among the most foolish, ineffectual and pathetic milquetoasts ever to have graced a cinema screen, but that, on a generous estimate, ninety percent of the celebrated talk is sheer, unadulterated twaddle. To the degree that I'm capable of recalling any line of dialogue whatever from his films (with the exception of his two literary adaptations, Kleist's *Die Marquise von O . . .* and Chrétien de Troyes' *Perceval*), I fear I would be hard pressed to quote a single specimen of genuine intelligence or wit.

Rohmer's ploy is a little like that of the poetess and *littérateuse* Anna de Noailles – when sashaying across a packed and glittering salon, she would startle her escort by suddenly spouting gibberish, but gibberish calculated to sound, from a distance, like a string of gracious, pearly epigrams. So brilliantly does he jingle and jangle the small change of wit that, just as his characters seem persuaded that they are making clever remarks, so most of his spectators seem persuaded that they are hearing them. (This is exactly what Hitchcock called 'directing the audience'.) He has in particular an extraordinary gift for parodying the lapidary speech patterns of classical French comedy, of Musset and Marivaux, with an especial affection for that ' . . . nothing but . . .' formula to which the more disillusioned of eighteenth-century aphorists were addicted: 'Women are nothing but the . . .', for example, or 'Sexual attraction is nothing but the . . .'. Needless to say, it hardly matters what tailpiece he attaches: the

*culturati* and would-be *culturati* are already nodding their heads in knowing, worldly acquiescence. And, somewhere out there, I suspect, as wily as the most famous character invented by his namesake Sax, Rohmer is chuckling over just how limpidly the vanity of the world on screen is mirrored by that off.

The brilliance and freshness of his work (his enchanting squib, *L'Arbre, le maire et la médiathèque,* might have been filmed by a man of twenty, except that no current twenty-year-old filmmaker has remained as young as Rohmer) is legendary, and justly so. Yet, for the reasons outlined above, I would argue that the finest of his films are those in which the language is as hesitant and imperfect as in everyday life. Such a film as *Le Rayon vert.* It is early August. Her holiday companion having abruptly stood her up, Delphine (Marie Rivière, who also collaborated on the script) finds herself in one French resort after another, conspicuously alone and lonely, saying *No!, No!* and *No!* again throughout the film – till, in the arms of the man for whom she has been waiting (the only man who will do, although she has never met him before), she sighs an ecstatically Joycean *Yes!* And even though there may be absolutely nothing existential about her solitude (when summer is over, she will doubtless be reunited with her community of friends), Rohmer somehow succeeds in investing it with a grandeur and an intensity equalled only by Rossellini and Ingrid Bergman. As with Bergman, too, Rivière's salvation demands nothing less than a miracle: the green ray, the tiniest and most moving special effect in the history of the cinema.

# 1987　Der Tod des Empedokles

## *The Death of Empedocles*

The problem with 'minimal' art is not that it's minimal but that it's not. The eye strays. Inside a cinema it's been trained to do so, often with aberrant results. (Although I doubt that I could coherently relate the plot of *North By Northwest,* a movie I must have seen four or five times, I believe I shall remember till my dying day the colour of Cary Grant's socks as he flees from the crop-dusting plane.) Even those films whose organization of visual stimuli within the frame is much sparer (those of the familiar 'transcendental' trio of Dreyer, Bresson and Ozu) frequently compensate for such spareness by an extreme sensitization of décor and accessories, so that a crude metal visor in Bresson's *Lancelot du Lac,* for example, becomes a rather more powerful focus of our attention than the face behind it.

The problem arises, as I say, with the kind of film which purposely offers the spectator less than what has come to be considered (but why and by whom and since when?) a normative amount of audiovisual information. It's not surprising that an audience weaned on the pinball pyrotechnics of *Star Wars* or the classical musak of a Kubrick soundtrack should find unutterably tedious the precision-tool framing of Jean-Marie Straub's (and his wife and collaborator, Danièle Huillet's) *Dalla nube a la resistenza* or be incapable of sitting still and listening to Gustav Leonhardt's playing of Bach in the same directors' *Chronik der Anna Magdalena Bach,* a film of monochromatic forms as austere but also as meaningful as the codified notations on lined music paper. The snag is that those of us who have been *cinéphiles* on and off since adolescence are hardly less vulnerable, and the deficiency has only been exacerbated by the currently assumed equation of the terms 'cinema' and 'spectacle', as equally by the immemorial bias against slowness of pace in the performing arts. (Not, though, in every art. After all, when we walk around a gallery to study its collection of paintings, our own natural, inner 'montage' may be as slow as that of the artiest of art movies, and audiences are certainly prepared to accept the equivalent of 'long takes' in the theatre.)

In any case, of all so-called minimal films, it's the Straubs' which appear to present the most formidable obstacles. It's widely believed, for example, that their films are essentially cerebral exercises, interesting for their 'ideas'. In fact, the ideas are always quite simple and straightforward in themselves, albeit long reflected upon; and if one's enthusiasm for *The Death of Empedocles* is based on the mere fact that Hölderlin's poetry (the film is an adaptation of an incomplete verse drama by the German romantic poet) has been allotted to voices untrained to speak it in the orthodox style, one might just as well have stayed at home and recited the play oneself. What matters, rather, is the *physical* presence of the text,

of the speaker, of his gestures as he delivers Hölderlin's lines, of the way in which his body moves in relation to the landscape and the frame, even of the impeccable cut of his toga as seen against the magnificence of the natural settings. *The cinema, in other words.* With one fundamental difference, however. We all learned a long time ago that great movies need not be bound by high-art values, standards or prejudices. Sternberg is a great director, even if his plots are an insult to the intelligence. Godard is a great director, even if his ideas are seldom more than Left Bank commonplaces. Ford is a great director, even if his heroines are ninnies. But in no film by Straub and Huillet is there anything to make allowance for. And this above all, I feel, is the unpardonable offence that has caused their work to be so marginalized.

There is, in another of their films, *Trop tôt, trop tard,* a lengthy, statically filmed shot of workers strolling in and out of a factory in Cairo. Patently a homage to *La Sortie des usines Lumière,* it also constitutes, for its directors, something of a manifesto. As Serge Daney wrote of it: 'the filmmakers, less meteorologists than acupuncturists, search for the spot – the only spot, the right spot – where their camera can catch people without bothering them. Too close, too far. Too close for them [the workers at the factory] not to see the camera, too far away for them to be tempted to go towards it. To find this point, this moral point, is at the moment the entire art of the Straubs.'

# 1988 Mujeres al Borde de un Ataque de Nervios

## *Women on the Verge of a Nervous Breakdown*

There isn't, but maybe there should be, an ancient Spanish proverb to the effect that 'Old men wear old hats out of which young men pull rabbits'. It would certainly apply to the movies of Pedro Almodóvar (or simply 'Almodóvar', as he affects to call himself, as if he were some sort of caped magician). For when his movies are written about, in particular that which remains his most-liked to date, *Women on the Verge of a Nervous Breakdown,* it's usually as a gorgeous patchwork of influences: Mexican melodramas; the black comedies of the now forgotten Spanish director Luis Berlanga; Buñuel, well-nigh automatically; Cocteau, somewhere; the pre-1968 Godard of fractured narratives and Day-Glo hues; the screwball comedies of Lubitsch, Wilder, Mitchell Leisen, Richard Quine and Blake Edwards; Pasolini, Fassbinder and Warhol, his three homosexual 'fathers', if I may put it thus; Minnelli and Cukor for the colour-coded 'look' of his visuals; finally, perhaps, the two Beatles musicals of Richard Lester.

That is, to be sure, already a potent cocktail, something of a Mickey Finn. There is, however, one influential predecessor to whom the director's exegetes have never alluded but who strikes me as possibly the most significant of all, his influence, moreover, being flagrantly detectable in the publicity still (opposite) for *Women on the Verge.* I mean Jean Negulesco and the CinemaScope movies he made in the fifties for Twentieth Century-Fox.

You must have caught one or other of them at some time, either *How to Marry a Millionaire* with Marilyn Monroe, Betty Grable and Lauren Bacall or *Three Coins in the Fountain* with Dorothy McGuire, Jean Peters and Maggie McNamara or *Woman's World* with Bacall again, June Allyson and Arlene Dahl or *The Best of Everything* with Joan Crawford, Suzy Parker and Hope Lange. They were 'women's pictures' at their most garish, most trivial and also most sexist, projecting their lurid glamour entirely through the supposed 'chemistry' generated by their (as a rule) three female stars. Yet although they were dismissed as worthless even by the director's former champions, it's still possible to entertain a certain indulgence towards them. For their own foolish sakes, first of all. But equally because they crystallized a precise moment of American culture and its sociomythology; in their own gaudy, unwitting fashion Negulesco's films arguably communicated as much of the truth of a culture and its dreams as did, for example, those of the *nouvelle vague.*

It was a culture as repressed and reactionary in its way as that of Franco's Spain, and the fundamental charm of Almodóvar resides in the ebullience with which he 'liberates' not only the society in which he was raised but the movies (Negulesco's included) which he consumed as an adolescent in that society. More specifically, as the modern cinema's most brilliant director of erotic scenes, he has given flesh to a number of long-suppressed homoerotic film-buff fantasies. If Godard had had a single gay bone in his body, so one imagines, he would have been Almodóvar. If Mitchell Leisen had had genius, he would have been Almodóvar. If Fassbinder had had a sense of humour . . . If Lester had had a drop of Latin blood in his veins . . . If Jarman had had talent . . . And so on. Because one can state categorically what, in the sacred canons of modernity, he is 'post', Almodóvar is the archetypal postmodern filmmaker.

Outside of his native land, however, his work continues to be received with a certain ironic condescension. In an era in which the pseudo-metaphysical, pan-European 'spirituality' of a Krysztof Kieślowski is treated as the *ne plus ultra* of intellectual filmmaking, Almodóvar is regarded as marginal, a born lightweight, a campy flibbertigibbet. Most damning of all, he is guilty of the cardinal offence of making us laugh. We laugh at his movies; alas (but it was ever thus), too many of us also laugh at the notion that they might be worth taking seriously.

189

# 1989  Do the Right Thing

You'll find the type just about everywhere these days, in Britain scarcely less than in the United States. I mean the Spike Lee type – small of stature, pugnaciously frail, shaving-brush crew-cut sprouting through a baseball cap worn back-to-front, expensive trainers and tight little granny glasses. The overall look is part pimp, part Rhodes scholar.

It's curious that, after Sidney Poitier and Bill Cosby and Richard Pryor and Michael Jackson, not to mention Martin Luther King and Adam Clayton Powell and Malcolm X and Jesse Jackson, it has been left to the runtish, near-nerdish Lee to set so distinctive a stamp on contemporary black street-style. (Among movie actors, only Eddie Murphy, teeth gleaming like a Cadillac's hub caps, has offered any serious competition.) Curiouser still is the fact that, as a performer in his own films, Lee has invariably cast himself as the protagonist's best friend – famously, the 'Ronald Reagan role'. And curiousest of all is that these best friends tend to be fecklessly scheming losers, drug-, gambling- and women-addicted, chronically out of their depth. Role models, though, have always been chosen from below, never imposed from above; and if the average white spectator has tended to remain a trifle ill-at-ease with Lee's professional persona, it isn't too hard to understand why his cool, cunning, cussed – in a word, spiky – presence has proved so appealing to youthful black audiences of the nineties.

The black celebrities who preceded him represented, in a way, the *regent* – ruling as best it could until the king attained his maturity. Poitier, Belafonte, Dorothy Dandridge and others of that generation were important in the forging of a crucial link between the droll if demeaning stereotypes personified in the thirties and forties by Hattie McDaniel, Butterfly McQueen and the generically named Stepin Fetchit and the advent in the eighties of such sassy, jive-talking superstars as Pryor, Murphy and Whoopi Goldberg. But it was Lee who, commandeering a space for himself both behind and in front of the camera, developing a public image that refused to be defined in relation (even hostile relation) to non-black needs, prejudices or expectations, ultimately ascended the throne. It was, I think, an authentic breakthrough.

Interestingly, even strictly as a director, Lee generates unease, causing him to be more esteemed than loved by white critics. Oh, he's a driven little calculator, is Spike Lee. Consider his career to date. With his first movie, the sexy *She's Gotta Have It* ('please, baby, please, baby, please, baby, please, baby'), he arrives with, as they say, a bang (commercial success, Cannes Festival, and so on). His second, the musical *School Daze,* appears slightly regressive and proves to be a critical misfire. Need to change tactics. *Do the Right Thing* – racial tension in Brooklyn's Bedford-Stuyvesant neighbourhood – establishes his

radical credentials (controversy, TV debates, etc.). Time out, maybe, for a more personal project, *Mo' Better Blues,* on jazz, arguably his finest, most poetic work, but destined to go the way of all jazz movies. Think again. *Jungle Fever* (miscegenation) – the Lee, once more, you love to hate. Then graduation to the Hollywood three-hour art movie and a black subject *par excellence, Malcolm X.* (Lee advises every black kid in America to play truant to see his film and markets 'X' as though it were a brand letter.) To no one's surprise, a commercial flop. So back to the populist drawing-board with *Crooklyn.* And so he goes, forever doing the right thing.

Or even consider a single movie – *Do the Right Thing,* precisely. Watch how he calculates and calibrates the agony. We have paid to see a movie advertised as being about racial violence, but for nearly all of its running time there *is* no real violence, just a shifting parade of potential suspects from one of whom, we trust, the violence we have paid to see will indeed flare up. But which one? And when? Lee keeps us guessing until we're all but *willing* the situation to explode, if only to relieve the tension at which he has so slyly contrived.

It is, when you think of it, exactly the same sadistically teasing construction exploited by Agatha Christie in the most celebrated of her whodunits, a novel to which *Do the Right Thing* bears rather an uncanny resemblance. I refer, of course, to . . . *Ten Little Indians.*

# 1990 Não, ou a vangloria de mandar
## No, or the Vainglory of Command

Although scarcely a strict measure, and certainly no guarantee, of any film's 'modernity', it's worth noting that what currently links many of the cinema's most innovatory artists is the fragmentation of their thematic pursuits, the dispersion of their energies in time and space, the apparent disinclination of their work ever to cohere into what is traditionally regarded as an oeuvre. The filmographies of Duras, Straub and Godard, for example, now look peculiarly cluttered in print, the former pair frustrating any neat categorical division into features, medium-length films and shorts (not forgetting, either, that the designation 'Straub' should rightly be 'Straub and Huillet'), the latter shaping up conventionally enough until the necessity, from 1968 onward, to include co-directors, the Dziga-Vertov Group and a lengthy video interregnum. Still more extreme is the example of Ruiz, whose fathomless filmography is, as I've already remarked, a veritable Rubik's Cube.

Strangest of all, however, is the case of the octogenarian Portuguese master Mañoel de Oliveira. Anyone who admired his first feature, *Aniki-Bobo*, back in 1942 would then have had to wait all of two decades for its successor, *O Acto da Primavera (The Passion of Jesus)*, to which it bears no resemblance whatsoever. The next film in the canon, a smooth, black, Buñuelian comedy, *O Passado e o Presente (Past and Present* – the *o* in these titles is not declamatory, merely the Portuguese word for *the)* came along in 1973 and the fourth, *Benilde ou a Virgem-Mae (Benilde: Virgin and Mother)*, two years after that. The fifth, which established him internationally, *Amor de Perdicão (Doomed Love)*, was premièred in 1978 and the sixth, *Francisca*, in 1980. Since when, uniquely in the medium, Oliveira has reversed the predictable, 'natural' course of a respectable career in the arts by making practically a film a year. These have included: a magnificent six-hour-plus adaptation of Claudel's nearly unstageable historico-religious drama *Le Soulier de satin (The Satin Slipper,* a film beautiful and moving – and this is not a paradox – even in its inevitable longueurs); an opera, half-Mozart, half-Buñuel, written directly for the screen, *Os Cannibales (The Cannibals)*; a three-hour paraphrase of the Bovary myth, *Vale Abraão (Abraham Valley)*; and *No, or the Vainglory of Command*, one of the greatest historical films ever made.

Nothing would be more futile than attempting to offer a pithy thumbnail sketch of Oliveira, a filmmaker who, if a national hero in his own country, is virtually unknown elsewhere – nothing would be more futile than attempting to convey in a few words his consistently sumptuous imagery, his theatricality, his

perversity, versatility and virtuosity. It's enough, perhaps, that his name is here, where it belongs. But it is at least important to locate wherein resides the precise originality of *No*. Seamlessly fluctuating from the past to the present, from dream to reality, from myth to history, from medieval romance to modern guerrilla combat, it contrives to embrace, as few films have done (it has been compared to *Intolerance*), an entire nation's collective memory, a collective memory centred upon four defining events of Portuguese history: the assassination of the Lusitanian rebel Viriatus in 139 BC, the death of Prince Afonso in 1490, the Battle of Alcaçar-Quibir against the Arabs in 1578 (of which the image above is an illustration) and the colonial struggle in contemporary Angola. And what all of these events have in common is that they were *disasters* – catastrophes for Portugal. A national destiny as an almost uninterrupted sequence of defeats: it is simply inconceivable that the cinema of any other country treat its own history with such lucid, limpid disrespect.

*No, or the Vainglory of Command* opens with a leisurely circular tracking shot around an enormous, screen-filling tree, its branches spreading out to the four corners of the frame like the fingers of a huge splayed hand, a hand that refuses to harden, to congeal, into a militant fist. *No!* it says to us, against all the gleefully reiterated *Yeses* of, say, American war movies (even those that complacently style themselves 'antiwar'). *No, no, no, no, no!*

# 1991 Dahong Denglong Gaogao Gua
## *Raise the Red Lantern*

Red. Red lanterns. Red walls. Red divans. Red-and-silver draperies. Red pyjamas. Red veils. There's one colour to which Zhang Yimou, the director of *Raise the Red Lantern* (and also of an earlier film, *Red Sorghum*), has an evident partiality. And thereby hangs something of a tale. This 'red', now the emblematic colour of Yimou's films, and perhaps of the new Chinese cinema in general, is not at all that of the Red Flag, of the Red Guard, of Mao Tse-tung's *Little Red Book* – not the red, in short, of what used to be known as Red China. Here is a novel, possibly unique, phenomenon in contemporary culture: to wit, the eroticization of what was once an exclusively political signifier, the *sexing* of the populist iconography of Chinese Communism and in particular of its characteristic hue. For Chinese films today are possessed of what can only be called an erotics, an erotics whose basic mythic ingredients are (aside from the colour red) the Peking Opera – perceived not only as a beleaguered bastion of classical Chinese culture but also as a campy sanctum of hetero- and homosexuality in a puritanical Marxist society – and the single word 'concubine'. (The title of the novel by Su Tong on which *Raise the Red Lantern* was based was *Wives and Concubines*; another prominent international success of the new Chinese cinema was Chen Kaige's *Farewell My Concubine;* yet another recent film featuring Yimou's own fetish-actress Gong Li was Stephen Shin's *The Great Conqueror's Concubine.*) That this is the current Occidental image of what used to be one of the most prudish cinemas in the world is nothing short of amazing.

All the same, and notwithstanding the difficulties that many of these filmmakers have experienced with the authorities of their native country, it's possible to find something rather dubious in the highly exportable chinoiserie (there is no other word) of their films, in the detectable whiff of nostalgico-colonial exoticism that they emit (an exoticism indistinguishable from that of Bertolucci's *The Last Emperor*), not least in the complacent lingering over the gorgeous golden-cage trappings of their put-upon heroines, all of which seem intent, consciously or not, on maximizing their appeal to sophisticated western palates. As it happens, the movie of which *Raise the Red Lantern* most reminded me was George Cukor's *The Women,* which, amusing as it is, has never been held up as an example of progressively feminist filmmaking. And Gong Li, the latest diva of the international film set, arguably belongs to a long tradition of sultry oriental houris that can be traced back at least as far as Anna May Wong.

With Yimou, as with several of his contemporaries, what is perhaps most

beguiling to western audiences is the return not to form (how many of us really know what the Chinese cinema used to be?) but to *forms*. These new Chinese films are consciously, even self-consciously, elegant artefacts. *Raise the Red Lantern* is, in fact, less a formalist than a 'formal' movie, 'formal' in the cramped Sunday-best sense of a 'formal occasion' or 'formal dress'. In lieu of any real and inventive compositional dynamics from shot to shot, it offers only a lazy, monotonous symmetry (practically every shot in the film is dominated by a conspicuously thrusting angle of perspective), so that, no matter where you're sitting in the auditorium, you always seem to have the middle seat in the very front row.

As an Oxford undergraduate, Oscar Wilde spoke languidly of the obligation that he felt to 'live up to' his blue china. Let me suggest, therefore, that the new Chinese cinema will not truly be new until Yimou, and filmmakers like him, no longer feel it incumbent upon themselves to live up to their red China.

# 1992 Unforgiven

In *Reflections on 'The Name of the Rose'*, the little volume that Umberto Eco wrote to explain the genesis of his best-selling novel, there is a brief essay on postmodernism from which I never tire of quoting. Eco defines the postmodern attitude in this way: 'as that of a man who loves a very cultivated woman and knows he cannot say to her, "I love you madly", because he knows that she knows (and that she knows that he knows) that these words have already been written by Barbara Cartland. Still,' continues Eco, 'there is a solution. He can say, "As Barbara Cartland would put it, I love you madly." At this point, having avoided false innocence, having said clearly that it is no longer possible to speak innocently, he will nevertheless have said what he wanted to say to the woman: that he loves her, but he loves her in an age of lost innocence. If the woman goes along with this, she will have received a declaration of love all the same.'

Sergio Leone's masterpiece, *Once Upon a Time in the West*, was the first postmodern western, a western for an age of lost innocence, a declaration of love to the American cinema. Filmed in Italy and Spain in 1968, within the cycle of the so-called spaghetti westerns, it presupposed in the spectator an impassioned affection for, and virtually limitless familiarity with, the thousands of Hollywood westerns that had both preceded and generated its existence. So much so, indeed, that its ostentatiously rhetorical title was something of a misnomer: 'Twice Upon a Time . . .' might more aptly have caught the spirit of the enterprise. For if there was nothing new in its three hours of running time, that was precisely the point. Leone's performers, too, if entirely convincing on a superficial level of narrative plausibility, gave what might be described as self-referential performances. None of them actually snarled, 'As John Wayne would put it, stick 'em up!', but, had any of them done so, it would not have struck a false note. *Once Upon a Time in the West* did not kill the western off, as was claimed by sentimental purists. Rather, in the sumptuous maestria with which it recapitulated the genre's themes, codes and conventions, it constituted a magnificent obituary.

But one thing that film history teaches us is never to write the obituary of Lazarus. Most of Clint Eastwood's early westerns (*The Outlaw Josey Wales, Pale Rider*) were in a postmodern, post-Leone mode: their settings, both natural and stylized, resembled nothing so much as a vast game reserve for that now endangered species, the American cowboy. What was extraordinary about *Unforgiven*, by contrast, was that it gave us a unique foretaste of what not only the genre in question but the American cinema as a whole might look like *when they re-emerged on the other side of postmodernism*. It was, in a sense, the first authentically *post*-postmodern Hollywood movie. Leone's baroque manners

and mannerisms, once sedulously mimicked, were now completely assimilated, thereby enabling Eastwood to return the western, its mythopoeic potency intact, to its proper habitat.

For years and years and years there existed, in the American cinema, stories, hundreds, thousands, of stories, guzzled up by filmmakers the way oil used to be guzzled up by sleek shark's-fin-winged Pontiacs and Cadillacs. Then suddenly, as also with oil, a crisis arose. Hollywood came to the painful realization that even it contained but a finite number of tellable tales and that, for its perennial renewal – indeed, for its very survival – it would have to learn how to conserve them. As might have been predicted, this conservation initially took the form of a *recycling*. Hence the wave, which has not yet receded, of prequels and sequels, remakes and premakes, by which the medium, like a constipated boa constrictor, has started to swallow itself.

Out of that wave emerged *Unforgiven*. It was not an especially innovatory movie. Nor, though, was it one which, like those of, let's say, *les frères* Coen, depended for its every effect on the public's knowing connivance. Eastwood had a good story to tell, and he told it movingly and powerfully, without once winking at the spectator as if to say, 'Hell, it's only a movie.' And what makes that some kind of an achievement is the mere fact that it can still be done – or done again. Hollywood, *it can be done*.

# 1993  Jurassic Park

This photograph is, or ought to be, startling. Why? Because there's a dinosaur in it. And dinosaurs don't exist. Or, if dinosaurs exist, then human beings don't exist. It ought to be startling, and yet of course it isn't at all, because it's merely an example of special effects, the sort of effects which infants are now familiar with, even jaded by, almost from the womb. It's an image from the most successful film ever made (at least as I write) by the most successful director who ever lived. So successful is Steven Spielberg that if he wants dinosaurs to exist, they exist. In his current position of absolute power he might have conjured anything into existence, but he chose the multi-million dollar schlock of dinosaurs. Again, why? Perhaps, to regard it indulgently, because of those 'childlike instincts' of his that he has so miraculously 'preserved', etc. Or perhaps, more cynically, because, in view of the subject's franchising opportunities, it allowed him to take to its logical conclusion the principle of all so-called 'product placement', by making a movie that is itself the product being placed.

If poetry is, as Marianne Moore famously defined it, an imaginary garden with real toads in it, then the reverse of that definition – a real garden with imaginary toads in it – should logically define the exact opposite of poetry. Whether that is in fact the case, it's certainly an accurate definition of *Jurassic Park*. By which is not intended an assault on a film that is in any event beyond the influence of any critic. (I readily accept that, where *Jurassic Park* is concerned, *I* am the dinosaur.) What is at issue here is not the quality of the film but only that of its special effects, effects that I seemed to be alone in finding disappointing.

That may appear a cranky criticism to offer of a film for which even its severest detractors had to concede an unprecedented level of supernatural verisimilitude. For me, however, it was just where the problem lay. The effects were so outlandishly seamless that in a paradoxical sense they quite failed to register *as* effects. When, in *Terminator 2*, the bad Terminator managed to elude Arnold Schwarzenegger's clutch by a self-generating act of instantaneous physical transformation, we were made witness to the effect itself. When, by contrast, the dinosaurs of *Jurassic Park* gave chase to their human quarry, they were so very 'realistic' it was, after the initial moment of astonishment, ultimately no more magical than watching a horde of marauding elephants pursue Lex Barker in some dreary Tarzan movie. The basic instant of transformation, between the imaginary (immemorially extinct dinosaurs) and the real (their convincingly alive presence on the screen), had taken place in the laboratory a long time before the movie began. What the spectator was given to see was, in effect, the *effect* of the special effects, not the special effects themselves. (The same remark might be made about the experience of watching Gary Sinise play a legless Vietnam veteran in Robert

Zemeckis' *Forrest Gump*. So persuaded are we, even if we know better, that the actor himself must be legless, we wholly fail to 'enjoy' the effect.)

What, surely, cinematic special effects should be all about is *metamorphosis* – as, precisely, in morphing, the computerized transformational process now so inexpensive it has become something of a televisual commonplace. Morphing continues to have unexploited possibilities in the realm of pure storytelling. (Just think of a morphed version of *Alice's Adventures in Wonderland*.) Equally, its advent may constitute the belated introduction into filmic grammar of the metaphor. (When, in *October,* Eisenstein juxtaposed a shot of a vainglorious Kerensky with that of a mechanical peacock, what he devised was a filmic simile, the visual equivalent of stating that one thing is *like* another; a metaphor, on the other hand, like morphing, cuts out the middle-man of *like*.) And it's possible to entertain a positively staggering speculation on its potential. If morphing can bend human features so easily to its will, might it not also lend expression to a face where none previously existed? Might it not, in short, be applied to the face of an inexpressive actor – a Tom Cruise, let's say, or (but probably this would be asking too much even of morphing) a Chuck Norris – and cause him, if only for the duration of a single performance, to become a good one?

# 1994 Ed Wood

There is, in Tim Burton's *Ed Wood*, the biography of a man, Edward Wood Jr, who became, as it were, *famous for being unknown*, for being, or so it's alleged, the worst director in the history of the cinema – there is, I say, a scene in the film in which Wood (the excellent Johnny Depp, uncannily reminiscent of Desi Arnaz's Ricky Ricardo in *I Love Lucy*), abetted by a geriatric, morphine-addicted Bela Lugosi (the extraordinary Martin Landau, uncannily reminiscent of the real thing), steals a mechanical octopus from the props department of Republic, the least impoverished of Hollywood's Poverty Row studios, for clandestine use in his own not just low-budget but practically no-budget epic, *The Bride of the Monster*. Unfortunately, albeit all too typically, once Wood reaches his nocturnal lakeside location, he discovers that he has omitted to steal the octopus's motor, without which it will be incapable of flailing and threshing with a semblance of conviction. Never mind. Lugosi will have to wing it. Wood seats himself beside his camera, Griffithian megaphone in hand. He cries out *Action!*, the 'Open Sesame' of all filmmaking, the inept as well as the ept. Lugosi, a game old pro, who has doubtless been here before, immerses his decrepit frame in the water and begins frantically to engage in a to-the-death combat with the muppety monster. *Cut!* The eternally optimistic Wood can barely contain his enthusiasm. And it *is*, on his part, nothing but sheer, blinkered optimism, for in the cold, black dawn of a cinema auditorium the struggle can only provoke derisive laughter. And yet . . . there is about it, too, in view of poor Lugosi's age and fatigue, a hint of genuine grandeur. For a brief moment at least, we too, like Wood, *believe*.

This, surely, is how true parody should work, as an expression of love as much as derision, legitimizing exactly that emotional and aesthetic presumption that laid the original so cruelly open to mockery. As belatedly as in a Pearl White serial, Burton rescues his eponymous subject from the jaws of everlasting contempt that already seemed to have closed about him. *Ed Wood* is a paradox, a film about a director who never had a success made by a director who has never had a flop, a sunny, good-humoured chronicle of failure and ignominy. And although it's a film about the cinema's past, which is why it was selected to bring to its conclusion this homage to the medium's first hundred years, it may equally be said to offer a lesson for its future. For it demonstrates that a mainstream film can still be made in which *conflict*, that immemorial motor of all drama, has not irrevocably degenerated into *violence*, a concept so similar, so utterly different.

It is, though, I repeat, a film about the past, one as richly referential as the book you are about to close. Think of it. It may have been Orson Welles' example that Wood sweated to emulate, but the material obstacles he had to contend with were those, rather, of an Edgar G. Ulmer, with whom, of course, Lugosi – whose most

indelible role was that of Browning's *Dracula*, itself influenced by Murnau's
*Nosferatu* – collaborated on *The Black Cat*, thereby anticipating the films made
by Tourneur under the capacious bat's wing of Val Lewton, themselves
descended in their turn from the work of Feuillade and, ultimately, of Méliès.
And just as it has been smoothly running forward, so the ribbon of film history
can be made to run backward to its source. Almodóvar's women step back from
the verge of their nervous breakdown; Aschenbach quits Venice in a reversely
gliding gondola; Kubrick's star child is re-endowed with humanity; Belmondo's
Michel Poiccard rises from the dead, dragging on his Gauloise; Ford's horse
soldiers return, cloppity-clip, cloppity-clip, across the Rio Grande; miraculously
re-forming itself, a glass paperweight springs up intact into Kane's cold, sweaty
palm; Eisenstein's Tsarist soldiery retreat in perfect formation down the Odessa
Steps; *Greed* gratefully expands into its full and pristine ten-hour splendour; and
the workers at the Lumière factory are sucked back into the darkness from
which they once so unforgettably emerged. Meanwhile, the wide screen
contracts to what is known as the Academy format and the cinema definitively
reverts, as it does in *Ed Wood*, to its black-and-white origins – the black-and-
white, precisely, of the printed page which you have just finished reading.

# Acknowledgements

I would primarily like to thank Howard Mandelbaum and the staff of PHOTOFEST, his amazing photo archive in New York City, without whose enthusiasm and erudition this book would simply not have been possible. I am particularly grateful to Ed Maguire, a senior member of that staff, who steered me through the forking paths of film history with unfailing patience and good humour.

I'm also deeply grateful to Catherine Fröchen of the photo archive of *Cahiers du Cinema*; to the Stills, Posters and Design department at the British Film Institute and to Theo Evans, who conscientiously trawled through its treasures on my behalf; to Sarah Harvey of the distribution company Artificial Eye; to the Kobal Collection; to the Swedish Film Institute; to Melanie Tibb and Erich Sargeant of the BFI; and to Michelle Sewell of Buena Vista International (UK).

In addition, I would like to acknowledge the guidance provided by Jay Leyda and Charles Musser's *Before Hollywood* (Hudson Hills Press), in relation to the very earliest years of the American cinema.

Finally, I wish to thank my editor, Walter Donohue, for being there when I needed him and for knowing when to edit and when not to edit: a rare gift; and my publisher, Matthew Evans, for commitment and enthusiasm beyond the call of duty.

Needless to say, what errors remain in this book, whether of fact or judgement, are mine alone, and I assume full responsibility for them.